SECOND LANGUAGE ACQUISITION

Also available from Bloomsbury

Issues in Second Language Proficiency edited by Alessandro G Benati

Key Terms in Second Language Acquisition, 2nd edition Bill VanPatten
and Alessandro G Benati

Language Acquisition and Language Socialization Claire Kramsch

Processing Instruction and Discourse Alessandro G Benati and
James F. Lee

The Grammar Dimension in Instructed Second Language Learning
edited by Alessandro G Benati, Cécile Laval and María J. Arche

*The Interactional Feedback Dimension in Instructed Second Language
Learning* Hossein Nassaji

SECOND LANGUAGE ACQUISITION

A THEORETICAL INTRODUCTION TO REAL-WORLD APPLICATIONS

Alessandro G Benati and Tanja Angelovska

Bloomsbury Academic
An imprint of Bloomsbury Publishing Plc

B L O O M S B U R Y
LONDON · OXFORD · NEW YORK · NEW DELHI · SYDNEY

Bloomsbury Academic

An imprint of Bloomsbury Publishing Plc

50 Bedford Square	1385 Broadway
London	New York
WC1B 3DP	NY 10018
UK	USA

www.bloomsbury.com

BLOOMSBURY and the Diana logo are trademarks of Bloomsbury Publishing Plc

First published 2016

© Alessandro G Benati and Tanja Angelovska, 2016

Alessandro G Benati and Tanja Angelovska have asserted his right under the Copyright, Designs and Patents Act, 1988, to be identified as the Authors of this work.

British Library Cataloguing-in-Publication Data

A catalogue record for this book is available from the British Library.

ISBN:	HB:	978-0-5671-0449-6
	PB:	978-0-5672-0019-8
	ePDF:	978-0-5670-7975-6
	ePub:	978-0-5671-1200-2

Library of Congress Cataloging-in-Publication Data

A catalog record for this book is available from the Library of Congress

Typeset by RefineCatch Limited, Bungay, Suffolk
Printed and bound in Great Britain

Table of contents

Illustrations

Figures

Tables

Acknowledgements

We would like to express our gratitude to all our students and colleagues in SLA for helping us to develop the ideas contained in this book. A special thank you to the anonymous reviewers who provided insightful comments, suggestions and overall feedback on its contents. Last but not least we wish to thank Lisa Carden, Lianna Iwanikiw, Gurdeep Mattu and Andrew Wardell at Bloomsbury for supporting us in this venture and producing this book as well as Stephanie Peter for her work on the index.

Preface

Why this book

This book has been written in order to help undergraduate students and trainee teachers to reflect on certain topics and key issues related to second language acquisition (SLA). Despite the proliferation of books and introductory courses on this topic, most of these very often provide an extremely complex account of associated theories and sometimes fail to emphasize the crucial interplay between how people learn languages and the most effective way to teach languages.

Thus the overall aim of this book is to provide an overview of SLA research and theories by identifying the main key issues in this field and by highlighting the classroom implications of this research. The study of SLA is rich and varied, conducted primarily by authors and academics whose interests and training often lie in the broader disciplines of linguistics, psychology, sociology and education. This book is informed by an increasing number of findings that have a direct application to classrooms and thus serve as a resource to inform teaching practice. Knowing how languages are learned will help language instructors develop a more innovative and effective way to teach foreign languages and to create the necessary conditions for students to learn more efficiently and appropriately.

Although the field has increased in size, scope and complexity in recent times, this book will attempt to simplify the main issues, questions and areas of controversies in the field. We will highlight what we know about second language acquisition and flag up the most salient strategies for language instruction and instructors. Readers will be encouraged to reflect critically on the presented content via a range of activities – including questions and related matching activities, choices and conclusions – all of which focus on how SLA theories can be applied in classroom situations and beyond.

How the book is structured

Our journey starts with some general definitions and considerations around the role of SLA.

Chapter 1 provides the readers with an overview of the various theoretical contemporary frameworks in SLA. A basic model of SLA is provided, key terms are defined and potential real-world applications suggested.

Chapter 2 offers an analysis of possible similarities and differences between the acquisition of a first and a second language. This is a fundamental issue in SLA theory and research. Key concepts such as universal properties, innate knowledge and transfer are introduced and analyzed. Different views around the role of universal properties, parameter resetting and transfer are presented, as is research on the possible role of age as a critical period in SLA.

Chapter 3 addresses key issues such as the role of input in SLA and the role of instruction and individual differences in the acquisition process. Input plays a vital role whereas that of instruction seems to be limited. Research on individual differences has investigated a number of variables such as motivation, age, working-memory capacity, aptitude, learning styles and learning strategies.

Chapter 4 deals with important issues related to the developing system of learners and language output. Theorists and researchers have attempted to explain how a language system develops and how learners might tap into it to access information for speech production.

Chapter 5 offers an explanation for how individuals learn to communicate in a second language, how they socialize and adapt to the rules of a particular speech community and what the communicative competence they are aiming to acquire consists of.

Chapter 6 provides a concise evaluation of what we know in SLA, highlighting the principal real-world applications and implications. Finally, the glossary provides the reader with a definition of key terms.

Introduction to second language acquisition

Introduction

This first chapter has four aims: to define the term second language acquisition (henceforth 'SLA'); to provide a brief account of main contemporary theories in SLA; to offer a basic model of SLA so that readers may understand its key elements; and to reflect on practical applications and implications of SLA theory and research. The latter has been conducted from different perspectives (linguistic, language universals, cognitive), and has attempted to shed light on the complexities of language growth and the role of a number of internal and external factors.

Despite the various and different theories and theoretical frameworks formulated in SLA, scholars have agreed the first language (henceforth 'L1') is the starting point and that when learning the second language (henceforth 'L2') learners must 'overwrite' its properties to create a new language system. This new system does not appear to be influenced or affected by instruction. Learners follow certain sequences and orders in the acquisition of another language. A number of factors (e.g. processability, frequency, redundancy and saliency, among others) are thought to be responsible for the emergence and acquisition of linguistic features.

Overall SLA is implicit. Language is a dynamic and integrated system that interfaces with input. Learners seem to make use of declarative working memory when they learn a lexicon and idioms, but they use procedural working memory for grammatical features. Input plays a crucial role in second language acquisition and provides the data for the internal processors. Output and interaction are also important, although output is constrained by processing. Taken in isolation, individual differences might not contribute towards providing us with an understanding of the internal processing responsible for acquisition; future research on these might focus on uncovering possible correlations between specific individual variables and SLA processes. We will give an overview of important theories below.

This chapter also outlines a number of real-world applications for instructors and instruction. Instruction needs to take into account each learner's internal system. Instruction's ultimate aim must be the development of implicit knowledge. Instruction should maximize exposure to language input, and needs to provide learners with a balanced combination of focus on form and meaning respectively.

Many questions about SLA remain unanswered, while others have had only partial responses to date. Indeed while the field has increased in size and scope, it is still sufficiently focused on questions of learning and teaching for many voices and perspectives to be acknowledged. The richness and complexity of SLA as a learning process and an area of study suggests that there are many perspectives to apply and many more applications to find. In the following chapters, the main questions and issues raised in SLA theory and research will be individually presented and analyzed.

A definition of SLA

SLA is a field of enquiry that has developed rapidly over the last forty years. Studies in SLA have investigated a number of phenomena using different participants (e.g. subjects with different first languages, different proficiency levels, different backgrounds, etc.), examining different contexts (e.g. formal and informal environments), and adopting a variety of research methods:

- experimental studies have manipulated a variety of pedagogical treatments and measured the learning outcomes. Experimental research is conducted in order to explore the strength of a relationship between variables. Scholars and practitioners are often interested in investigating the effects of factors such as a particular 'teaching technique' on language learners' performance or processing.

- observation studies have generated a number of important questions about individuals and groups to be investigated by researchers. Classroom observation is an ideal methodological framework to systematically investigate teaching, learning issues and processes in a second language classroom context. Classroom observation (i.e. action-research framework) is used in second language research for different goals: to compare language teaching methods; to explore effective classroom pedagogical approaches; and to evaluate teachers and materials.

- case studies have examined the language produced by teachers and learners in classroom contexts. A case study is not a standard methodological package like an observational study or an experimental study, but rather examines the way in which a one-off event occurs. A case study normally considers data from different sources, examines an issue/problem in real-life contexts and uses SLA theory to generalize the main findings.

The field of SLA is also becoming more interdisciplinary, and now draws on methods from research areas such as psychology, neurology and education in order to shed light on how learners develop a new language system.

What is second language acquisition?

Name three areas/topics of research in SLA you have come across in your reading.

1

2

3

SLA is the study of how learners create a new language system despite an often limited exposure to the second language/foreign language learning contexts. In a general sense, a second language (L2) refers to a language that is acquired after the first language (L1) has been established in early childhood. If we look at the various definitions of SLA, what emerges is a concern about learners and learning. Researchers in SLA are mainly interested in exploring the processes involved in the acquisition of an L2 and the internal and external factors that might affect acquisition.

SLA addresses two fundamental questions:

1 how learners come to internalize the linguistic system of another language;

2 how learners make use of that linguistic system during comprehension and speech production.

SLA can be equated to the construction of building, as understanding SLA 'is like understanding how a building works. There is the electrical system, the plumbing, the foundation, the frame, the heat and the air system, and so on. All are necessary; one alone is insufficient. But like those who work in house construction and are electrical contractors or plumbing contractors, in second language acquisition some of us are in matters dealing with input. Others are interested in output.' (VanPatten 2004: 27).

SLA consists of a series of theories, theoretical views, hypotheses, frameworks and generalizations about the way in which L2 learners create and develop a new language system. Recent reviews of second language acquisition theories (cf. Atkinson 2011; Robinson 2012; Ortega, Cumming and Ellis 2013; Benati 2013) have attempted to group various theoretical perspectives along a kind of continuum, ranging from rationalist and linguistic, to cognitive, psycholinguistic and sociolinguistic positions with the intention of understanding some of the processes and mechanisms involved in the acquisition process:

- from a rationalist perspective, humans have an innate capacity to develop language and we are genetically programmed to develop our linguistic system in certain ways. This view is/was in strong opposition to that espoused in behaviourism, which maintained that it is the learner's experience that is largely responsible for language acquisition and indeed is more important than any other capacity.
- understanding SLA from the linguistic perspective of SLA focuses on the language dimension and the linguistic system underlying the grammar and construction (competence) of L2.
- from a cognitive perspective, we need to know how the human brain processes and generates new information. Cognitive theorists are concerned with how L2 learners access the linguistic knowledge in real time or the strategies they might use to do so.
- psycholinguistic approaches to the study of SLA focus on how L2 learners process information, organize their knowledge and subsequently use it.
- from a sociolinguistic perspective, variation and changes in specific elements of the learner's L2 linguistic knowledge are caused by a number of social factors such as social setting, task, communicative purpose, learner intention, role and identity.

Researchers need to continue investigating SLA from these different perspectives before we can develop a complete picture of how languages are learned and the mechanisms and processes responsible for this.

What do you think are the three main factors responsible for language acquisition?

1

2

3

Research into SLA has laid the groundwork for a number of important findings, but despite fast-growing interest in the topic, there remain debates and controversies over some of its key issues and this is partly due to the complexity and the multifaceted character of the field. Studies have increased in quantity as researchers have addressed a variety of topics, set new questions and worked within multiple research methodologies and from a variety of academic disciplines (e.g. linguistics, applied linguistics, psycholinguistics, psychology and education). As a result of this multidisciplinary work, we are in a better position to argue that learners acquire a second language through a number of interactive factors, namely: exposure to language input; making use of existing knowledge of the native language; and accessing universal properties. Some of the main claims are:

- L2 learners create an implicit, integrated and dynamic system residing in the brain. This system exists outside awareness.
- L2 learners make use of both procedural and declarative working memory systems to process, storage and retrieve information.
- input provides the raw data for the language system to develop and grow.
- the acquisition of grammar is a linguistic and processing constraint and it is a function of the learner.

Issues still up for debate – and related questions – include:

- Is the acquisition of L2 similar or different to that of L1?
- What are the main characteristics of language growth?
- What are the roles of input and output in second language acquisition?
- What is the role of individual differences?

The nature of language

What do we need to acquire in a language? Learning a language means processing a number of elements:

- lexicon – the vocabulary within a language, specifically the total stock of words, word elements and their meanings.
- phonology – the study of sound patterns. It also refers to the sounds that make up words (pronunciation), and the way they come together to form speech and words.

- morphology – how words are formed. Morphology describes the patterns of word formation (inflections on verbs and nouns) and how new words are made from other words (prefixes and suffixes).
- syntax – the rules of sentence structure. Syntax explains what is permissible – and what it is not – in a target language.
- pragmatics – the use of sentences to intend something specific. It refers to the role of context in language and how people rely on it for successful communication.
- sociolinguistics – the study of the language and how it functions in society. Sociolinguistics is the study of the interaction between linguistic and social variables, such as when it is appropriate to use different types of language.
- discourse – the way sentences are connected. Discourse is essentially about how coherent and cohesive linguistic elements are in sentences.

Acquiring a language, then, means acquiring all these elements. As you might expect, acquisition is a complex phenomenon, and the knowledge picked up by children for their L1 is not necessarily available to L2 learners.

Activity

Match the linguistic terms with the synonyms

Syntax	Vocabulary
Discourse	Grammar
Lexicon	Sounds
Morphology	Word structure
Sociolinguistics	Connecting sentences
Pragmatics	Appropriate use of language
Phonology	What the speaker meant by a sentence

Theories in second language acquisition

Theories in SLA have been developed in the attempt to understand how L2 learners come to develop their competence in a second language. Research into first language acquisition has also provided good insights into the processes involved in the acquisition of a second language. A great deal of the theorizing about SLA has been undertaken with language learning and language learners in mind, and includes:

- Behaviourism
- Universal Grammar Theory
- Monitor Theory
- Interaction Hypothesis
- Processability Theory
- Input Processing Theory
- Skill Acquisition Theory
- Emergentism
- Declarative and Procedural Model
- Complexity Theory
- Sociocultural Theory

Behaviourism

The behaviourist theory that prevailed in the 1940s and 1950s was supported by psychologists such as Skinner (1957). The theory made a number of claims, including that:

- human learning and animal learning are the same;
- the child's mind is a *tabula rasa*; there is no innate knowledge;
- all behaviour is viewed as a response to stimuli;
- behaviour happens in associative chains.

Language was seen by behaviourists as a progressive accumulation of habits and the goal was error-free production. The L1 was seen as a major obstacle to L2 acquisition since it caused interference errors (caused by habits in the L1) and negative transfer (from L1 to L2) of habits.

Contrastive analysis (Lado 1957) was an approach to the study of SLA based on a close comparison of L1 and L2 to understand and identify the similarities and differences between the two in terms of phonology, morphology and syntax. The concept of positive and negative transfer is central to the contrastive analysis and behaviourism. Positive transfer occurs when learners transfer a structure that is appropriate and similar in both languages, while negative transfer happens when learners use a L1 structure inappropriately in the L2. The easiest L2 structures to learn are the ones that also exist in learners' L1 and have the same form and meaning. Corder (1967) questioned the assumption that learners' errors are the result of 'bad habits'. In fact, only a small percentage of errors made by learners in the L2 are traceable to the L1. Instead errors are 'a window' into the learner's mind. Errors show important insights into learning processes and learners' language development, but behaviourism could not explain these underlying processes.

Within the behaviourist framework, theorists believed that language learning involves acquiring verbal habit formation. Learners proceed from form to meaning; that is, they first master the grammatical forms and then move on to express meaning. Certain conditions were applied for acquiring these habits:

1 the learner imitates and repeats the language heard;

2 the imitation has to be rewarded;

3 as a result of this, the behaviour is strengthened, reinforced and eventually becomes habitual.

Name the two main implications of behaviourism for language pedagogy.

1

2

Universal Grammar Theory

The Universal Grammar (UG) theoretical framework applies Chomsky's theory (1975) to the study of second language development (White 2003, 2015). One of the key claims of this theory is that languages are a complex and abstract system which develops in the human mind. Chomsky (1965) argues that humans possess innate knowledge of language universals (UG) and principles which regulate the acquisition of languages. These are modified and corrected according to the input to which humans are exposed. Researchers within this theoretical framework have been concerned with how languages are represented in the mind (mental representation of language) and how learners come to know more about a language than what they have been exposed to ('poverty of the stimulus'). The theory makes a number of claims:

● learners have their own internal syllabus (abstract principles) to follow, and these constrain the acquisition of both L1 and L2. The information contained in our mind (innate universal grammar system) influences the development of a second language (interlanguage development).

- learners make projections about the language they learn that are often beyond the information they are supposed to know (poverty of the stimulus). In other words, they sometimes know how a linguistic feature works, what is grammatical or ungrammatical without having been exposed to that particular feature (as tested by grammaticality judgment tests).

> What are the two main implications of the UG Theory for language pedagogy?
>
> 1
>
> 2

In the UG Theory, the role of the language instructor is reduced from that of someone who structures the learning path to the person who presents the 'linguistic data' to which learners react and that they manipulate in order to develop their mental representation of the target language. Language instructors should provide learners with good linguistic input which interacts with their internal/innate grammar. The input learners are exposed to should help them reset their internal abstract principles to account for language variations. So, for example, L1 English learners would need to modify the principle that language is 'head initial' (SVO *Alessandro speaks Japanese*) to the principle of 'head final' (see Chapter 2 for the different hypotheses on the availability of UG) when learning Japanese (SOV *Alessandro Japanese speaks* or OSV *Japanese Alessandro speaks*). All humans possess universal features of language which constrain the acquisition of grammar, but one key question within this theoretical framework is whether learners at different stages of their lives have the same or different access to their UG system(s).

Monitor Theory

Krashen's Monitor Theory (1982, 2009) suggests that L2 learners acquire language mainly through exposure to comprehensible input in a similar way to how they acquired their first language. The main prerequisite for this is that learners are exposed to comprehensible and message-oriented input. The key concepts of the Monitor Theory are as follows:

- grammatical features are acquired by L2 learners in a specific order ('order of acquisition') regardless of their L1. Morphological features, such as the progressive (-*ing*) in English, are acquired (no matter what the learner's L1) before the regular past tense (-*ed*) or irregular past tense forms, which are acquired before third-person singular (-*s*). Instruction is therefore constrained by a universal and predictable order of acquisition (morpheme studies).

- when learners acquire a second language, they develop two systems that are independent of each other. The 'acquisition system' (unconscious and implicit) is activated when we are engaged in communication. By contrast the 'learning system' (conscious and explicit) functions as a monitor and corrector of our production.

- it is paramount that learners are exposed to comprehensible input that is slightly above their proficiency level (*i*+1) and learn their L2 in a relaxed environment that enhances their motivation (and consequently their output).

- learners who are comfortable and have a positive attitude towards languages will have low barriers to language learning and typically respond well to their instructors. By contrast, stressful environments in which learners are forced to produce before they feel ready to do so will raise their filters and block their processing of input.

What are the two main implications of the Monitor Theory for language pedagogy?

1
2

The Monitor Theory has pedagogical implications for language instruction and language instructors and was translated into a methodology to language teaching called the 'Natural Approach'. In a nutshell, it suggests that language instruction should focus on providing learners with a rich variety of comprehensible input (*i*+1) and opportunities to use language spontaneously and meaningfully. The input that L2 learners receive should be simplified with the use of contextual and extra linguistics clues (e.g. gestures, pictures, drawings, etc.). Grammar instruction, in a traditional sense, does not have any impact on language acquisition according to the Monitor Theory. Second language acquisition is similar to first language acquisition as learners make use of the same acquisition faculty in their brain. A great deal of acquisition happens incidentally and naturally when learners are exposed to input and engage in interactions which focus on meaning.

Interaction Hypothesis

The Interaction Hypothesis was originally developed in the early 1980s. This theoretical framework focuses on how interactions might affect acquisition with the view that input is a key ingredient for the acquisition of a second language. It explores how such interactions might affect acquisition in essentially two ways: first, by modifying input; and second, by providing feedback related to the linking of meaning and form (Gass and Mackey 2015). Through these interactions, learners have the advantage of being able to negotiate meaning and make some conversational adjustments. Input modifications occur when the other speaker adjusts his or her speech due to perceived difficulties in learner comprehension or to provide corrective feedback. This Interaction Hypothesis makes the following claims:

- 'input' refers to the language learners are exposed to (positive evidence), and it is an essential element for learners to make linguistics hypothesis. There are two types of input: interactional and non-interactional. Interactional input occurs when there is some kind of communicative exchange involving the learner and at least another person (e.g. conversation, classroom interactions, etc.); non-interactional input occurs in the context of non-reciprocal discourse that does not involve the learners (e.g. announcements).

- interaction plays an important role in second language acquisition. Language modifications can help learners notice things they would otherwise overlook, and picking up on certain linguistic features in the input can have an effect on acquisition. How learners are led to notice things can happen in several ways, including input modifications, such as comprehension checks (*'Is this clear?'*, *'Do you understand what I mean?'*) and clarifications requests (*'What did you say?'*, *'Can you say that again, please?'*, *'What does it mean?'*).

- the negotiation of meaning in conversations or interactions refers to a communication breakdown between two speakers (native speakers and/or non-native speakers) and the subsequent adjustments made to facilitate comprehension.

- corrective feedback (negative evidence) is used when one speaker indicates to another that what he or she has produced isn't quite right. The feedback can either be direct or indirect. When given direct feedback, the learner is told explicitly that his or her utterance is incorrect (*'We don't say it that way. We say . . .'*, *'You forgot to put the past tense marker on'*, etc.). In the case of indirect feedback (or indirect negative evidence), one speaker implicitly points out that something is wrong by recasting the sentence with the correct form.

(For example, 'I goed to the park'. 'Oh, you went to the park. And what did you do?') Unlike direct corrective feedback, indirect negative evidence does not normally interrupt the flow of communication and is focused on meaning. Interactions that elicit feedback can thus have a facilitative role in language acquisition.

- 'output' refers to the language learners need to produce in order to express meaning. It can play a number of roles: it can help learners pick up on linguistic or grammatical points through interactions, or it might help the formulation of hypotheses about the target language that learners can test during language production.

> What are the two main implications of the Interaction Hypothesis for language pedagogy?
>
> 1
> 2

The Interaction Hypothesis has clear implications for language pedagogy. For example, it suggests a new classroom dynamic in which instructors and learners take new roles and responsibilities, and highlights that comprehensible and message-oriented input and interactions play key roles in the acquisition of a second language. Moreover learners and instructors are engaged in a number of interactions (whether clarification requests, confirmation checks or comprehension checks) that facilitate language acquisition. The hypothesis also emphasizes the importance of developing a new definition of communication which should take into account both the acquisition of the target language's linguistic properties and its application in everyday life. Output practice should help learners to use the target language for a specific purpose and intent rather than simply learning by rote. Grammar instruction might be beneficial if it is provided by enhancing the input through the use of different techniques (e.g. input enhancement, textual enhancement), and could have a facilitative role in helping learners pay attention to the formal properties of a targeted language without the need for metalinguistic discussion.

Processability Theory

The Processability Theory is a theory of language development which accounts for how learners develop and use certain output processing procedures to string words together in speech production (Pienemann 1998, 2007; Pienemann and Lenzing 2015). These procedures emerge over time in a particular order and cannot be skipped by learners. According to this theory, learners process information unconsciously and (for example) they assign words to specific linguistic features (e.g. *Alessandro* is assigned to the lexical class called 'noun' and the feature 'singular', *speaks* is assigned to the lexical class called 'verb' and the features 'singular-present-non continuous'). In this case, grammatical information needs to be exchanged in order to achieve subject–verb agreement. The theory also holds that learners' output processing procedures emerge over time in a predictable order. Learners acquire single structures (i.e. negation, question formation) through set stages. Instruction is constrained by these developmental stages, and L2 learners in particular follow an especially rigid route in their acquisition of grammatical structures, as any given stage assumes knowledges of the steps prior to it. In the case of the acquisition of question formation in English, six developmental stages have been identified (see Table 1.1. below). In Stage 1, learners use single words to ask questions. In Stage 2, learners use intonation following a subject–verb–object (SVO) structure. In Stage 3, the use of Wh-/Do emerges. In Stage 4, learners can use copulas, while in Stage 5 they use the auxiliary in second position in direct questions and overgeneralize this in indirect questions. Finally in Stage 6, learners learn to understand statement word order in indirect questions.

The theory's variation dimension accounts for the existence of interlanguage varieties within each of the processable structures. Due to a range of interlanguage varieties among learners the same structure might appear in different forms. For example some use target-like forms as well as non-target-like forms; some may use a different word order rule to others in varying linguistic contexts; some may struggle to apply any structure at all.

Table 1.1 Sequence of acquisition for English question formation

Stage	Description	Example
1	Use of words	Yes?
2	Use of SVO	You like Italy?
3	Use of Wh-/Do?	Do you like it? What you like?
4	Use of inversion	Where is my book? Have you seen it?
5	Use of auxiliary in second position (direct and indirect)	Where can she go? What did he do?
6	Cancel inversion	I wonder where he is

The Processability Theory makes two main claims:

1 the theory supports the view that SLA can be broken down into stages. L2 learners can only produce the linguistic forms for which they have acquired the necessary processing capacities. If a learner is at stage 3, he or she cannot produce – in a coherent fashion – grammatical structures that require the procedures at stages 4 and above. As noted above, learners follow a very rigid route in the acquisition of grammatical structures, and these structures become learnable only when the previous steps on this acquisitional path have been reached.

2 learners might display individual variation with regard to the extent to which they apply developmental rules and how they acquire and use grammatical structures.

What are the two main implications of the Processability Theory for language pedagogy?

1

2

One of the main real-world implications of this theoretical framework is that the role of instruction is limited and constrained by L2 learners' readiness to acquire a particular structure. Instruction might be detrimental to acquisition if it does not consider learners' current developmental stage, and instructors must therefore consider learners' psycholinguistic readiness as appropriate in order to be effective.

Input Processing Theory

The Input Processing Theory (VanPatten 1996, 2014) refers to how learners perceive and detect formal features of language input, and the strategies or mechanisms that guide and direct them to comprehend what they hear or read. When learners are exposed to the target language input, only a small portion of that input is processed and becomes intake. This is due to two main factors: first, our limited capacity to process information; second, the use of processing strategies to cope with the amount and type of information that the mind has to work through.

Research on input processing has attempted to describe the linguistic data that learners attend to during comprehension and the data they eschew, for example what grammatical roles learners assign to nouns or how a word or phrase's position in an utterance influences what gets processed. These principles are one explanation of what learners are doing with input when they are asked to comprehend it.

The theory makes two main claims:

1 learners seem to process input for meaning (words) before they process it for form (grammatical features). In a sentence such as 'Yesterday I watched my son playing in the park' – which contains a lexical feature encoding a particular meaning (temporal reference 'yesterday') – learners will tend to process the lexical item (Yesterday) before the grammatical from (–ed) as they both encode the same meaning. This is due to the use of processing strategies which causes learners to skip grammatical features in the input and causes failure in mapping one form to one meaning.

2 learners parse sentences in order to figure out who did what to whom, thereby relying on word order and employing a first noun processing strategy that assigns subject or agent status to the first noun or pronoun they encounter in that sentence. For example, in 'Paul was kissed by Mary', learners might assign the role of agent to the first noun or noun phrase in the sentence and therefore misinterpret the sentence, thinking that it was Paul who kissed Mary. This can cause delay in the acquisition of syntax.

What are the two main implications of the Input Processing Theory for language pedagogy?

1

2

Manipulating the input might help learners to process grammar more efficiently and accurately. This theory has important pedagogical implications for second language instruction. Grammar instruction, for example, should be aimed at changing the way input is perceived and processed by language learners. Learners can be exposed to meaningful input that contains many instances of the same grammatical meaning–form relationship (e.g. the verb ending –ed encodes a past event). An approach to grammar instruction which moves from structured input to structured output practice is likely to help learners to connect meaning to grammatical forms (the intervention is called 'processing instruction').

> What is the main difference between the Input Processing Theory and the Processability Theory?

Skill Acquisition Theory

The Skill Acquisition Theory (DeKeyser 2007, 2015) relates to a cognitive and information-processing model centred around three stages of development: cognitive, associative and autonomous. According to this model, SLA is generated by exposure to input and the ability of L2 learners to process information and to build networks of associations. SLA entails moving from a controlled mode of operation (declarative knowledge) to automatic mode (procedural knowledge) through repeated practice. This theory addresses issues related to the way people develop fluency and accuracy: accuracy refers to the ability to do something correctly while fluency refers to the speed with which a person can do something. Theoretically, accuracy and fluency can develop independently of each other, meaning that someone could be highly accurate but exceedingly slow at doing something, or exceedingly fast but highly inaccurate. In reality, however, research on skill development has shown that the two tend to develop in tandem: as accuracy increases, so does speed. Another important concept of the Skill Acquisition Theory is the role of explicit or implicit learning in acquiring grammatical rules, but this is very much dependent on the complexity of the rule. Simple rules can be learned explicitly while more challenging ones may be more effectively acquired implicitly.

The two main claims made by the Skill Acquisition Theory are:

1 learning begins with declarative knowledge (information is gathered and stored) and slowly becomes procedural (people begin to be able to use that knowledge in practice). Declarative knowledge involves the acquisition of isolated facts and rules (e.g. knowing that a car can be driven); procedural knowledge requires practice and involves processing longer units and increasing automization (e.g. knowing how to drive a car).

2 the theory applies only to those learning situations where the following four criteria are met: adult learners are of high aptitude; structures are simple to be learned; learners are at fairly early stages of learning; and the context is instructional.

What are the main two implications of the Skill Acquisition Theory for language pedagogy?

1

2

This theory views SLA as a process which entails going from controlled mode (declarative knowledge) to automatic mode (procedural knowledge) through repeated practice. Learners need to be taught explicitly and need to practice the various grammatical features and skills until they are well established (fluency).

Emergentism

Emergentism is cognitive theory that accounts for how learners develop language abilities and competences (Ellis 2007; Ellis and Wulff 2015). According to this theory, SLA is governed by the same type of processes and principles that underpin all other aspects of human knowledge. Emergentism holds that acquisition is a dynamic process in which a number of elements (such as regularities, frequencies, associations, L1, interactions, the brain, society and cultures) operate and are responsible for the emergence and development of the second language. The theory makes two main claims:

1 language acquisition is an implicit process in which frequent input plays a key role. The two other constructs important for language performance are recency (recent events, things) and context.

2 language and its properties emerge over time and result from the way in which simple cognitive learning mechanisms interact with data gleaned from the learner's environment.

As part of this process, language instructors should expose learners to form (either linguistic, metalinguistic or pragmatic) to help them get to grips with their new language system.

What are the two main implications of emergentism for language pedagogy?

1

2

According to this theory, frequency and regularity are key factors in language acquisition. Acquisition is the result of a learner's interaction with his or her surrounding environment. As noted above, emergentism holds that language and its properties emerge over time and are the result of cognitive mechanisms interacting with input, the implication being that it is better for the language instructor to expose L2 learners to real and natural settings so that they can increase their knowledge. The more knowledge learners gain of their target language, the more interaction they initiate and become involved in.

Although the role of grammar instruction is limited and it is not always effective, emergentism argues that it can have a facilitative role in developing the 'noticing' of target forms which might not otherwise be salient in the input language.

Declarative and procedural model

This theoretical model derives from neuroscience theory and research and examines brain activities to explore issues related to language learning and language processing. According to Ullman (2015) there are two independent (but in some cases overlapping) memory systems in the brain: declarative memory and procedural memory. Declarative memory is mainly responsible for the acquisition of vocabulary or stock phrases, while procedural memory is used for implicit learning of grammar.

This model makes a number of interesting claims, particularly about declarative and procedural memory. Although humans use both types when they acquire languages, each has a specific role. For example, we rely on declarative memory for learning vocabulary and irregular morphology, and also use it initially to work with regular (that is, predictable) grammatical information. Procedural memory is then relied on for the acquisition of more challenging grammatical forms and structures.

What are the two main main implications of the Declarative and Procedural Model for language pedagogy?

1
2

One of the main implications for language instruction is that neither learning nor practising grammar rules is likely to promote spontaneous use of those rules. Learning words and meaning-bearing phrases, however, may lead to spontaneous grammatical utterances.

Complexity Theory

The Complexity Theory (Larsen-Freeman 2002, 2015) is mainly concerned with the behaviour of dynamic systems that evolve from chaos into order. Unlike the interlanguage model of SLA, a complex model creates its own conditions of development in open interaction with its environment, and is always susceptible to change. The main claims of this theory are:

1 SLA is not characterized simply by processing and internalizing data. The system is more complex than the acquisition of a set of rules and features and it is crucial to understand how learners use linguistic knowledge and how that is influenced by context.

2 interaction with the environment, the context, and the variability of learning outcomes among L2 learners are key features of this theory. Which of these aspects are strengthened and which are weakened within the dynamic system depends on who L2 learners interact with and on the environments they find themselves in.

3 language components interact with the L2 system through a meaning-making process.

> What are the two main implications of the Complexity Theory for language pedagogy?
>
> 1
> 2

According to this theory, language instructors should throw the language system into initial chaos out of which will emerge a system that is in alignment with the target language. The complexity theory supports the importance of learners' exposure to input and a social participation view of SLA, without excluding the psycholinguistic perspective, and therefore provides us with a wider perspective towards SLA research, theory and pedagogy without offering any explanation about how the learning system emerges.

Sociocultural Theory

Sociocultural Theory argues that the development of human cognitive functions derives from social interactions. It is the participation of individuals in social activities which draws them into the use of these functions. The theory focuses not only on how adults and peers influence individual learning, but also on how cultural beliefs and attitudes impact instruction and learning. The central constructs of the theory are:

1 mediation. Mediation refers to the idea that humans possess certain cultural tools, such as language, literacy, numeracy, that they purposefully use to control and interact with their environment.

2 the zone of proximal development (ZPD). The ZPD refers to the distance between a learner's current ability to use tools to mediate his or her environment and the level of potential development. In short, the ZPD is a metaphor to describe development situationally.

3 the verbal thought. Language acquisition concerns language function development, mental function development and the combination of language and thought. Generally speaking, it includes the process that the low level external or social speech develops into the highest-level inner speech or 'verbal thought'.

Sociocultural Theory makes a number of basic claims:

1 all learning or development takes place as people participate in culturally formed settings, such as schools, family life, peer groups, workplaces, and so on. These environments shape the most important cognitive activities in which people engage. Thus, all learning is situated and context-bound. Social interaction plays a crucial role in the process of cognitive development. In this context social learning precedes development.

2 the highly knowledgeable participant – someone who has a keener understanding or stronger ability – can create learning conditions conducive for the novice learner and thus play a fundamental role in helping the less knowledgeable learner's language development.

3 learners use tools like speech and writing to mediate their social environments. These tools differ between individuals and the situations in which they find themselves, and they also have certain limits, such that people use them only in certain ways.

What are the two main implications of the
Sociocultural Theory for language pedagogye?

1

2

A clear application of the Sociocultural Theory's principles to language instruction can be found in the form of Task-Based Language Teaching, which emphasizes the importance of social and collaborative aspects of language acquisition and how the interaction between learners can scaffold and assist in the L2 acquisition process. Sociocultural Theory (Lantolf, Thorne, and Poehner 2015) regards instruction as crucial to L2 development in the classroom and holds that it should be geared to the ZPD just beyond learners' actual development level. The theory also suggests that during instruction (metalinguistic and explicit), learners develop an awareness of the structure and function of language by using it socially. Their environment provides the context and assists in the understanding of the language's grammatical properties.

Although SLA research and theory do not provide a uniform account of how acquisition happens – and particularly how instruction can best facilitate language acquisition – clear progress has been made in gaining a better understanding of the processes involved in acquiring another language and developing effective classroom teaching, and a set of generalizations for second language teaching can be drawn. These might might serve as the basis for offering real-world applications for instructors and instruction (see Chapter 6).

Activity

List the five key claims for SLA and explain their importance.

1

2

3

4

5

Activity

Complete the following table.

Language acquisition happens through/by/if	According to which theory?
exposure to the language as a complex system of units is built and the units become interconnected in the learner's mind.	
only if the condition $i+1$ has been fulfilled.	
through chaos . . .	
learners are taught how to perceive and process linguistic data appropriately by mapping the form and meaning.	
overlapping memory systems.	
'comparing' their innate knowledge of language with the structure of the particular language.	
cognitive development, including language development, which arises as a result of social interaction and a supportive interactive environment.	
using the linguistic symbols together in patterned ways.	
developing a certain level of processing capacity in the L2 before they can use their knowledge of the features that already exist in their L1.	
exposure to thousands of examples of language associated with particular meanings . . .	
through corrective feedback during interaction and 'negotiating for meaning'.	

Activity

Match the key theories with the main theorist.

- Behaviourism   Gass
- Universal Grammar Theory   Krashen
- Monitor Theory   Ulmann
- The Interaction Hypothesis   DeKeyser
- Processability Theory   Pienemann
- Input Processing Theory   Lantolf
- Skill Acquisition Theory   VanPatten
- Emergentism   Ellis
- Declarative and Procedural Model Larsen-Freeman
- Complexity Theory   Chomsky
- Sociocultural Theory   Skinner

A model for SLA

Entailing as it does the acquisition of different systems (e.g. phonological, lexical, morphological, syntactical, etc.), SLA is complex. It also consists of a number of mechanisms/processes (e.g. input processing, intake, accommodation and restructuring, output, output processing strategies to access information, etc.) which are responsible for how L2 learners are able to process the characteristics of the new language and eventually tap into this new system for language production. A proposed model of SLA is one that moves from input processing to output processing.

INPUT → INTAKE → INTERLANGUAGE SYSTEM → OUTPUT

We now define and discuss the key constructs of this model.

Input and intake

Input refers to the language that L2 learners are exposed to, either by hearing or reading, and which has a communicative intent. Features in language (e.g. vocabulary, grammar, pronunciation, etc.) make their way into a L2 learner's language system only if they are linked to some kind of meaning and are comprehensible to that learner (see Chapter 4 for a full discussion on the role and characteristics of input). Input is considered a key ingredient of SLA, but for it to be effective and useful for learners, it must have two main characteristics:

1 L2 learners must be able to process it and to understand its meaning (not all the input will be picked up automatically by learners.

2 L2 learners might have to be exposed to modified input so that they can better comprehend the speaker's meaning (conversational interactions, clarifications and negotiation of language input can facilitate acquisition).

Intake (originally coined by Corder 1967) is the language that actually makes its way into a learner's internal system. Input is processed but not all of it will be converted to intake, for a number of reasons – including limited working memory capacity, memory, internal processing mechanisms, some internally driven aspects of grammar and so on – that we will address in subsequent chapters.

Scholars have agreed that acquisition will not occur (even if with input at the right quantity and quality) unless it is internalized by the learners and becomes part of their interlanguage system. SLA occurs when learners understand input that contains grammatical forms that are at a higher level than the learners' current interlanguage. However, as noted above we know that only *part* of the input is processed and passed in the form of intake into the developing system and eventually into output by the learner. Changing the way L2 learners process input and enriching their intake might therefore have an effect on the developing system, and this in turn may impact on how they produce the L2. According to the Input Processing Theory, when learners attend or notice input and comprehend the message, a form–meaning connection is made. Developing L2 learners' ability to map one form to one meaning is essential for acquisition. In the Interaction Hypothesis, input is also seen as a significant element/factor for acquisition without which learners cannot acquire a L2. Input can thus be regarded as absolutely essential to the SLA process and there is no related theory, view or hypothesis that does not recognize its importance. However, the question is: is input by itself sufficient for SLA? It is likely that some forms or structures cannot be acquired through exposure to input alone, and it has been suggested that a number of other factors might affect the acquisition of linguistic constructions, including: the frequency and saliency of features of forms in oral input; their functional interpretations; and the reliabilities of their form–function mappings. Therefore, one of the possible conclusions here is that while input is vital for acquisition, more is required than exposure to it.

Developing System

L2 learners develop an internal linguistic system called 'interlanguage' (Selinker 1972). As can be deduced from the name, this system is neither the first language nor the second language, but rather something in between that learners build from environmental data. Another key phrase relating to interlanguage is 'developing system', which refers to a dynamic and changing system that is an implicit and an unconscious representation of the language (e.g. morphology, phonology, syntax, etc.). It is a complex and continuously evolving unit comprising: networks of forms and lexical items that are linked to each other via semantic relationships (e.g. sad and funny); formal relationships (e.g. interesting and interested); lexical relationships (e.g. interesting and interest); and syntax (e.g. SVO, NP-VP-AdjP, etc.) that governs sentence structure and tells learners what is possible (and what is not) in a target language. These relationships are accommodated in the system in the early phases of learning but subsequently restructured (see Chapter 3 for a full discussion on the developing system).

How the system develops and the main factors that affect its growth have been discussed over the years. The behaviourist view (Skinner 1957) considered language acquisition as the training of habits. Contrastive Analysis assumed that errors made by L2 learners could be traceable to their L1s. Behaviourism became untenable after Chomsky's (1959) acquisition arguments, and research findings showed that many of the predicted errors (error analysis) did not occur and could not be explained on the basis of L1 transfer (Corder 1981). A number of theorists believe that human beings are born with an inbuilt disposition to language acquisition. A child possesses knowledge of language universals (UG) and generates from that knowledge a series of hypotheses about the particular first language he or she is learning. These hypotheses are modified and corrected in the light of the input to which the child is exposed. From this innate perspective L1 acquisition is primarily characterized by two factors:

1 an innate internal mechanism (language acquisition device). Universal Grammar consists of principles and parameters that provide children with (unconscious) innate knowledge of what is impossible in human language in general.

2 the input children are exposed to in their environment.

When L2 learners process language, they gradually incorporate the linguistic properties of the target language into the new language system via a process called 'accommodation'. This process affects further changes within the new system without the learner realizing it ('restructuring').

SLA research has focused a great deal on interlanguage grammatical development. For example, morpheme accuracy order studies have indicated that L2 learners follow an order of acquisition regardless of their L1. The consistency of the morpheme order led to the view that SLA was a matter of 'creative construction', and an implicit learning experience based not on rule knowledge but rather on an innate capacity for L2 acquisition.

Developmental stages studies on question formation have demonstrated that the acquisition of questions involves multiple stages. The first is characterized by the use of single words and formulaic expressions (e.g. 'Car? What's that?'). In the second stage, L2 learners use declarative word order. In the third stage, fronting of *wh-* words and 'do' begin to appear (e.g. 'What it is?' 'Do he like the food?'). By the fourth stage, inversion of *wh-* in copular questions begins (e.g. 'What is it?' 'Who are you?'), while the fifth stage is characterized by the appearance of inversion in questions that require do-support to lexical verbs (e.g. 'Do you like John?' 'Who is talking on the phone?'). In the final stage complex and less frequently used forms emerge (e.g. question tags).

Developmental sequences in L2 learners' acquisition of tense and aspect, both of which involve the acquisition of morphological features, have been studied intensively in SLA in more recent years. Research into these issues lend strong support to the existence of developmental patterns in L2 acquisition.

It appears that L2 learners create linguistic systems in a systematic and dynamic way that do not seem to be affected to any great extent by external forces such as instruction and correction. Researchers and theorists view SLA as a largely implicit process, principally guided by the learners' interaction with L2 input internally ('behind the scene'). There is a long-standing debate on whether acquisition is exclusively an implicit and unconscious process or rather, in some cases, the product of an interface between explicit and implicit knowledge.

- the implicit-unconscious view is sometimes referred to as the 'non-interface position'. According to this theory, explicit learning about an L2 is possible, but remains separate from the underlying competence in the target language that L2 learners eventually acquire. This position is consistent with nativist perspectives drawn from theories on linguistic universals.

- the 'strong interface position' argues that explicit L2 knowledge, attained through explicit learning, can become implicit L2 knowledge. This is generally achieved through practice in which learners deliberately focus their attention on L2 form (as it encodes message meaning) and work towards understanding and internalization. SLA is viewed as a skill, and its acquisition as a linguistic system is assumed to be built up gradually through processes of attention, conscious awareness and practice. Two types of knowledge are distinguished: declarative knowledge and procedural knowledge. In this view acquisition begins with declarative (e.g. information about the language rules) and slowly becomes proceduralized (acquired by performing a skill) through practice.

- the 'weak interface position' questions how much explicit learning and explicit instruction might influence implicit learning, and has identified possible limitations for instruction. Supporters of this position assume that SLA is predominantly implicit.

However, a linguistic system can be also built up through a number of instructional interventions that enable learners to pick up on crucial relationships of L2 form and meaning in the language input and eventually process these form–meaning mappings.

Output

'Output' refers to the language that learners produce and which has a communicative purpose. Through language production (oral and written), L2 learners acquire new knowledge and consolidate or modify their existing knowledge. Comprehensible input might not be sufficient to develop native-like grammatical competence alone, however, and thus learners also need 'pushed output', speech or writing that prompts them to produce language correctly, precisely and appropriately. Producing target language might encourage learners to pay attention to the constraints or grammatical structures of the target language and convey their own intended meanings in speech production. Several roles have been assigned to output (Swain 1995), namely that:

- output practice helps learners to improve fluency;
- output practice helps learners to check comprehension and linguistic correctness;
- output practice helps learners to focus on form;
- output helps learners to realize when the developing system is faulty and therefore notice a gap in their system;
- output creates greater automaticity, which is one pedagogical goal in SLA. Little effort is required to execute an automatic process as it has become routinized: one example might be the steps involved in walking towards a bike, getting out the key, unlocking the bike, pushing it, mounting it and riding it. Over time, this process requires little thought and can be done quickly.

The ability to produce forms and structures in output does not necessarily mean that forms and structures have been acquired, however. We need to distinguish between output as interaction with others and output as practice of forms and structures. Learners' implicit systems develop as they process the input they receive. Output promotes noticing of linguistic features in the input and conscious awareness of language and language use. It can also provide additional input to learners so that they can consolidate or modify their existing knowledge. The role of output is important – it promotes awareness and interaction with other learners – but it does not seem to play a direct role in the creation of the internal linguistic system. Conscious presentation and manipulation of forms through output practice might help L2 learners to develop certain skills in using particular forms or structures correctly and accurately in controlled tasks, but it does not seem to have a significant impact on the development of the implicit system responsible for acquisition. Output processing, though, involves the ability to make use of the implicit knowledge available to L2 learners to produce utterances in real time.

Activity

Key Issues in SLA

Read the following statements. Do you agree or disagree?

1. First and second language acquisition are similar.

   Agree   Disagree

2. Language development is affected by both explicit and implicit knowledge.

   Agree   Disagree

3. Input and Output have a similar role.

   Agree   Disagree

4. Individual differences (such as motivation) play a key role in SLA.

   Agree   Disagree

Real-world applications

Theory and research in SLA emphasize the complexity of acquisition processes. The following insights into language acquisition might be useful in developing an effective language teaching approach:

1 the internal and implicit processes responsible for language acquisition are similar regardless of learners' first language. Learners

process grammar often following a natural order and a specific sequence (i.e. they master different grammatical structures in a relatively fixed and universal order and pass through a sequence of learning stages).

2 learners require extensive exposure to second language input in order to build their internal new linguistic systems. Input needs to be easily comprehensible and the message oriented in such a way that it can be processed effectively by students. Research has shown that learners focus primarily on meaning when they process elements of the new language.

3 interaction with other speakers is a key factor in promoting acquisition.

4 acquisition requires learners to make form–function connections (the relation between a particular form and its meaning/s).

5 in the view of most researchers, the acquisition of a second language is primarily a matter of developing implicit knowledge.

6 language acquisition requires opportunities for output practice. Production serves to generate better input through the feedback that learners' efforts at production elicit.

Language instructors should aim to develop a principled, evidence-based approach to language teaching based on their knowledge about language acquisition theory and research. This approach should take the concept of communication (which is the interpretation, negotiation and expression of meaning) as a point of departure and feature the following characteristics:

- instruction needs to be predominantly directed at developing implicit knowledge that takes into consideration the orders and stages of development in learners.

- instruction needs to provide learners with comprehensible, simplified, modified and message-oriented input. Instruction should focus on providing opportunities for the learners to use language spontaneously and meaningfully. Corrective feedback in the form of recasting (implicit feedback, e.g. reformulating wrong utterance with the correct form) could provide more opportunities for input exposure.

- instruction needs to create opportunities for interaction and the negotiation of meaning among speakers. Learning is fostered when a communication problem arises and learners engage in resolving it using these approaches.

- instruction needs to provide opportunities to focus on grammatical form within a communicative context. Grammar approaches that promote learning are: input flood, textual enhancement, consciousness raising and structured input practice.

- instruction must provide learners with an opportunity to participate in communicative tasks – such as roleplaying and storytelling – that help them develop implicit knowledge and take responsibility for communication.

- instruction must create opportunities for learners to communicate by performing communicative functions (output). Whenever learners produce language, it should be for the purpose of expressing some kind of meaning. Meaning should be emphasized over form.

Acquisition involves the creation of an implicit system. Input, interaction and output are the cornerstones of language acquisition and the development of communicative abilities.

Where to find more about this topic

Atkinson, D. (ed.) (2011). *Alternative Approaches in Second Language Acquisition.* New York: Routledge.

Benati, A. (2013). *Issues in Second Language Teaching.* Sheffield: Equinox Publishing.

Benati, A. (2015). *Second Language Research: Key Methodological Frameworks.* Sheffield: Equinox Publishing.

Gass, S. M., and Selinker, L. (2008). *Second Language Acquisition: An Introductory Course.* New York: Routledge.

Robinson, P. (ed.) (2012). *Routledge Encyclopedia of Second Language Acquisition.* New York: Routledge.

Ortega, L. (ed.) (2015). *Second Language Acquisition* (2nd ed.). London: Routledge.

Ortega, L., Cumming, A., Ellis, N. C. (eds) (2013). *Agendas for Language Learning Research.* Malden, MA: Wiley-Blackwell.

VanPatten, B., Benati, A. (2015). *Key Terms in Second Language Acquisition* (2nd ed.). London: Bloomsbury.

VanPatten, B., Williams, J. (eds) (2015). *Theories in Second Language Acquisition* (2nd ed.). Mahwah, NJ: Lawrence Erlbaum Associates.

Similarities and differences between first and second language acquisition

2

Introduction

In this second chapter, the main similarities and differences between L1 and L2 acquisition will be presented. The question of whether L1 and L2 acquisition are similar or different processes is fundamental in this field of enquiry. The reader will be introduced to important topics, such as innate knowledge of the learner, Universal Grammar, Chomsky's innatist position, initial state for L2 acquisition, Fundamental Difference and Similarities Hypotheses and the constraints inherent within the process of acquiring a second language (transfer and markedness). The extent to which the factor of age may account for any differences and the potential confounding factors will also be discussed. The last section of the chapter extends the SLA discussion to the field of third language acquisition.

The starting point (universal properties – innate knowledge – transfer)

Chapter 1 provided a short description of the theory of Universal Grammar (UG). This theory argues that humans possess an innate knowledge of language universals or universal grammar (UG) and principles, which then regulate the acquisition of languages. These universal principles are modified and altered in response to the input to which humans are exposed. The starting point for language learners refers to the concept of the initial state, or what learners bring with themselves before they start acquiring a target (non-native) language.

Chomsky searched for an explanation for the fact that under normal conditions, all children acquire their first language even though they have not always been exposed to 'perfect' input (e.g., slips of the tongue, false starts, incomplete sentences, etc.) and they do not always receive systematic feedback. He found the explanation by arguing that children have a mechanism (language acquisition device) that guides them in the acquisition of their first language, a device later referred to by Chomsky as Universal Grammar (UG). UG is said to consist of general principles, applicable and common to all natural languages. When approaching the 'task' of learning a language, the samples of the language to which children have been exposed serve as the trigger needed for the activation of UG, and UG's principles then prevent children from making the wrong hypotheses about the acquisition of their first language. This innate knowledge allows them to discover the rules of the language system (Chomsky 1981; White 1989, 1996; Lightbown and Spada 2013) without any delays. In other words, this abstract knowledge governs the acquisition of the target linguistic system.

Observe a child learning his/her first language in your environment. Think about the input to which the child is exposed and the feedback he or she gets (if any), and try to highlight some evidence which supports the position that children are guided by UG in learning their first language.

1
2
3

The following evidence (Lightbown and Spada 2013) supports Chomsky's innatist position:

- children successfully learn their native language/s at a time in life when they would not be expected to learn anything else so (cognitively) complicated.

- children may show different levels of achievement in the areas of vocabulary, creativity, social skills etc., but they all achieve mastery of the structure of the language spoken around them.

- children come to know language rules and patterns that they have not been exposed to previously. They learn to manipulate input on their own, whereas animals (even primates receiving intensive training) cannot be trained in this kind of manipulation.

- children acquire their first language successfully even when they do not receive feedback. For example, rules on reflexive pronouns are innate and governed by universal principles, and they can be accessed and learned only through the application of abstract principles.

Yet although the UG theory has been accepted as a plausible explanation for L1 acquisition, the debate about whether it also applies to L2 acquisition is ongoing. The main controversy revolves around two questions:

1 Is UG applicable to L2 acquisition?

2 If so, for how long do learners have access to the universal principles when learning another language?

No SLA theory or research framework supports the view that learners start the process of acquiring a second language with no linguistic knowledge in their minds, i.e on a *tabula rasa* basis. All theorists believe that there is 'something' there, but the description of that something varies according to different positions (see also VanPatten and Benati 2010: 11). One view is that L1 might serve as an initial state in SLA (the 'transfer position'), while another holds that universal properties govern SLA processes (the 'non-transfer position').

There are three possible views in regard to the availability of UG to L2 learners:

1 the No UG Access Hypothesis (Bley-Vroman 1990; Epstein, Flynn and Martohardjono 1996) states that the L2 acquisition is different from L1 acquisition and it is not constrained by UG. UG is not responsible for L2 acquisition and the acquisition process is generally seen as a problem-solving one.

2 the Full UG Access Hypothesis (White 1985, 1989, du Plessis *et al.* 1987, Schwartz and Tomaselli 1990) states that UG is available to L2 learners and L2 acquisition is constrained by UG. The fact that L2 learners follow certain universal principles which work differently in the target language than in the learners' first language is seen as evidence that L2 learners still have access to UG. According to this view L2 learners might possess a knowledge of parameter-setting different to that in their L1, indicating that the option to set new

parameters might still be available to them. Flynn (1996) gives an example from L2 learners of English with L1 Japanese. Japanese and English have different settings in relation to the 'head parameter'. Japanese is a head-final language (SOV) – the verb occupies the final position in a sentence, while English is a head-initial language (SVO), where the verb is found before the object of the sentence. Thus, Japanese speakers who are L2 learners of English would need to reset this 'head parameter' to head-initial, although their L1 Japanese parameter is committed to head-final.

3 According to the Partial Access Hypothesis, UG is only partially available to L2 learners. L2 learners transfer just a limited portion of the L1, perhaps something from the lexicon and its properties, but might not carry across the functional features (e.g. agreement) of the L1.

We will now look more closely at the question of 'transfer' (also labelled as 'mother tongue influence', 'interference' and 'cross-linguistic influence').

Linguistic constraints (transfer and markedness)

Two linguistic constraints known to influence SLA and the self-organization of the interlanguage are the concepts of transfer and markedness.

Transfer

Transfer is definitely one of the most difficult concepts to be defined in the field of SLA. In terms of direction, transfer can be native language (L1) transfer, interlanguage transfer (transfer from L1 into L2) and reverse transfer (transfer from L2 into L1). Transfer can be either positive (facilitative, arising from similarities between languages) or negative (hindering acquisition, arising from differences between features of the languages under question). There are four main approaches to the nature of language transfer: process, constraint, strategy and inert outcome. Transfer seen as a constraint implies that within the language's development, learners make non-target-like productions because they make hypotheses for which they are constrained and influenced by the L1. According to Odlin (2003) a constraint prevents a learner from being or becoming aware of similarities. Transfer can be said to be dependent on two main factors: the exposure to input from the environment; and use and self-organization.

Think about the possible positions that differ from each other with respect to the roles they attribute to L1 transfer and access to UG and fill in the following table.

Type of transfer/access	Transfer from L1?	Access to UG?

There are six partially overlapping positions (see Table 2.1.), which differ from each other with respect to the roles they attribute to L1 transfer and (direct) access to UG:

1 Full Transfer/Full Access: all properties of the L1 constitute the initial state of SLA and UG fully constrains SLA.

Table 2.1 Transfer and access to UG

Type of transfer/access	Transfer from L1?	Access to UG?
Full	The initial parameter settings (and principle inventory) are transferred from L1. L1 is the starting point or the initial state of SLA.	UG fully constrains SLA.
Partial	Some, but not all, of the parameter settings (and principle inventory) are transferred from L1.	SLA is only constrained by those UG properties that do transfer.
None	The initial parameter settings (and principle inventory) do not depend on the L1.	UG is not involved at any stage of SLA, neither indirectly via the L1 or directly.

2 Full Transfer/No Access: all properties of the L1 constitute the initial
   state of SLA and UG constrains the subsequent development only via
   the L1.

3 Partial Transfer/Full Access: only parts of the L1 are transferred and
   UG fully constrains SLA.

4 Partial Transfer/No Access: some, but not all properties of L1 are
   transferred and L2 will only be constrained by those UG properties
   that do transfer with the L1.

5 No Transfer/Full Access: the L1 is not the learner's initial starting
   point about the L2 (no transfer) and UG fully constrains SLA.

6 No Transfer/No Access: UG is not involved at any stage of SLA,
   either indirectly via L1, or directly.

Three positions have been developed to explain how L2 learners approach
the task of learning an L2 and as to whether they rely on L1 knowledge or
not:

L2 learner transfer (all or parts of their L1) and reset parameters

A number of scholars believe that all the properties from the L1 are transferred
into SLA (e.g. Schwartz and Sprouse 1996; White 2003) and that L2 learners
replace L1 properties with appropriate L2 properties (full transfer) in a
process called 'parameter resetting'. Spanish is a null-subject language, i.e. it
allows a free omission of subject pronouns. Thus, the sentence *'Habla mucho'*
(without 'el' / 'he') is perfectly fine. English, on the other hand, is a non-null-
subject language and 'Talks a lot' (i.e. a sentence starting with a verb and with
an omitted pronoun would be not possible, as 'he' is required). Similarly, in
Spanish there are sentences where a null subject is required and where an
overt pronoun is not possible to be used at all. For instance, the sentence *'Es
imposible'* (English translation: 'it is impossible'). Hence, L1 Spanish
speakers will begin the acquisition of English by unconsciously assuming
that English has null subject properties, just as Spanish does, and therefore
believe that a sentence like 'Is impossible' (without the pronoun 'it') is
perfectly fine. Similarly, L1 speakers of English who begin acquiring Spanish
would initially believe that a sentence like *'Ello es imposible'* is fine. In both
cases, the learner will have to reset to the appropriate parameter (− null
subject or + null subject) during acquisition.

Other scholars believe that only some properties from the L1 are
transferred; the idea of partial transfer refers to L2 learners transferring parts
of their L1 in a limited manner. For example, Vainikka and Young-Scholten

(1996) claim that learners transfer the lexicon and its syntactic properties from the L1, but L2 learners do not transfer the functional features of a language. Syntactic properties refer to word order and valency of a verb, i.e. how many arguments a verb requires in order for the sentence to be grammatical; the verb 'give' requires three: a giver; something to be given; and a receiver of the thing being given. Functional features refer to things such as person–number agreement, tenses etc.

Not all investigations of interlanguage follow the tradition of attributing target-deviant structures to transfer from the L1. Pienemann's Processability Theory (Pienemann 1998; Pienemann and Lenzing 2015), instead sees some target-deviant structures as part of the developmental acquisition sequence for the second language, as evidenced by all learners of that language without any difference to their L1 background. According to the Processability Theory, even if a logical attribution of target-deviant structures in the L2 to the L1 is possible, the source will not necessarily be transferred. Learners move through certain developmental stages, which cannot be skipped: if learners are not developmentally ready to acquire a certain grammatical feature, they will not be able to process it either. The Processability Theory does not exclude the possibility of transfer, but holds that only a grammatical feature that is processed can be transferred.

> Can you think of a method that could identify transferred and/or developmental errors?

There are two principal ways of identifying transferred and developmental 'errors'. The first involves collecting instances of interlanguage data from L2 learners of different L1 backgrounds. If L2 learners from different L1 backgrounds produce the same interlanguage errors for the target structure, then transfer will not be the most likely explanation. The second involves comparing the 'errors' produced by L2 learners with those produced by children who acquire the target language as their L1. If similarities between L2 learners and children acquiring the target language as L1 are found, then the source of the 'errors' in the L2 interlanguage is probably not transferred from their L1.

L2 learners do not transfer but they do set parameters

According to this position, L2 learners begin SLA just as they acquired their first language. More precisely, L2 learners approach the task of acquiring an L1 with their universal guiding mechanisms and do not carry forward any pre-knowledge from the L1 that might influence the process of acquiring an L2. This is in accordance with the 'no transfer' position, which posits that learners approach the task of SLA as a completely new experience and rather than re-setting the existing parameters, they will simply set new ones according to the type of evidence they receive (in the example discussed above, it would mean that learners would either set their parameters to + null or − null subject).

L2 learners neither set nor re-set parameters

The third position observes the process of SLA as being completely different from the L1 acquisition process, qualitatively speaking. The main difference lies not in the presence or absence of UG, but rather in the parameterization. In other words, UG principles which are not subject to parameterization are available in both L1 and L2 learning processes, but the parameterized UG information is not directly present in the process of L2 learning. In contrast, in SLA learners employ *inductive* learning strategies, because the learning mechanisms/modules for L1 acquisition and SLA are different. Since the parameters are seen as part of the language module, neither parameter setting nor re-setting can occur (Clahsen 1988; Clahsen and Muysken 1989). They based their results on data gathered from learners of German as a second language and the feature in question was word order. In regard to the question of transfer, they assume a very minor role for transfer from L1 to L2. In their results, Clahsen and Muysken (1989: 14) found no direct transfer of word order L1 patterns in early-stage L2 learners and hypothesized that L2 learners have only indirect access to UG.

Markedness

First used in a phonology context, the notion of markedness was later extended to morphology and syntax. In SLA, markedness refers to the possible occurrence (or absence) of the transfer phenomenon and the 'ease' or 'difficulty' of certain phenomena. For example, in the case of two specific phonemes, they will be distinguished by the presence or absence of a single distinctive feature and based on that, one of the phonemes is said to be marked and the other one unmarked (/b/ is marked and /p/ unmarked with respect to voicing). Unmarked features are those that are universal or are present in most languages and which learners tend to transfer. Marked features are language-specific features and learners usually resist transferring them. An example from morphology would be *-ed* for past tense ('walked') versus the regular verb: the past tense verb will be marked by the suffixation of *-ed* and the present ('walk') will be unmarked. Often the morphologically unmarked form occurs more frequently but has a more restricted meaning than a morphologically marked form. For example, whereas the past tense form in English definitely refers to the past, the present tense form is more neutral with respect to temporal reference. The concept of markedness is quite widely accepted and it has been applied at all levels of linguistic analysis.

Two current approaches attempt to clarify the concept of 'markedness': the typological approach and the transformational approach. According to the typological approach, the marked language structures are more easily learned and processed than marked ones. Thus, 'if a marked category A always implies the presence of the unmarked B, a child must acquire B before, or simultaneously with A' (Greenberg 1991: 38). According to the transformational approach, core grammar rules (structures, sentences) – unmarked – are acquired in a relatively short time in comparison with peripheral rules (sentences, structures) which are marked.

Markedness is applied to understanding which features can be transferred. Other rules such as word order are innate, governed by universal principles and accessed through the application of abstract principles of language structure. Only the unmarked features can be transferred. This can be best illustrated by a simple example from English and Spanish (taken from VanPatten and Benati 2010: 11). When it comes to learnability grounds (White 1985, 1989), we can say that the [+ null subject] is the marked value and [− null subject] the unmarked value. So in the example discussed, [− null subject] is the initial, unmarked value of the parameter for Spanish learners of English and if learners are exposed to positive evidence that null subjects are permitted, the unmarked value [− null subject] can be re-set. Spanish learners of English will find it hard to abandon their L1 value [+ null subject] in favour of the English [− null subject] value, because initially learners are not exposed to positive evidence informing them that null subjects are not possible in English. The properties of the L1 are not only labelled as parameters. Depending on various theories, under 'properties of the L1' linguists may understand form–function relationships, processing strategies (how learners map form onto meaning) or parsing routines (i.e. how learners make syntactic relationships online while they are listening or reading).

The Fundamental Difference Hypothesis vs The Fundamental Similarities Hypothesis

Think of three characteristics that make L2 learners different from L1 learners.

1
2
3

When discussing the differences between L2 and L1 learners, we may conclude that:

- L2 learners are more cognitively mature (they possess problem-solving skills and make use of conscious attention).

- L2 learners already know at least one language.

- L2 learners have highly variable motivations for learning a second language.

These conclusions imply that differences can be found not only between L1 and L2 learners, but also between children and adults. To build upon the positions to UG access discussed in the previous section, it is important that we make ourselves familiar with the Fundamental Difference Hypothesis (or FDH; Bley-Vroman 1990).

Fundamental Difference Hypothesis

The FDH argues that the acquisition processes of children and adults differ fundamentally in terms of each group's 'innate ability'. Children possess the innate ability to acquire the L1 grammar, but adults lose this and as a result use problem-solving skills and conscious attention to acquire a target language. Hence, in terms of UG access, according to the FDH children have an access to UG and are guided by its principles and parameters, whereas adults no longer have direct access to it. Adults rely on general problem-solving abilities that help them consciously to infer the grammatical structures of the L2 input. Success depends very much on how well those problem-solving skills are deployed, and stand in stark contrast to the uniform and successful first language acquisition displayed by children.

FDH claims that adults have an indirect access to UG through their L1 grammar which helps them to use their L1 knowledge to develop their L2 interlanguage. In contrast to children, adults are not able to re-set their L1 parameters. According to the FDH, differences between L1 and L2 learners include the following:

- adult L2 learners' interlanguage will show more instances of transfer from L1 to L2 than child L2 acquirers.

- child L1 learners will produce non-target features with decreased frequency as their exposure to target input increases and they will level out abruptly within the native-like range (the end state, i.e. the point when the parameter is set). In contrast, adult L2 learners will continue to produce non-target structures.

Robert Bley-Vroman (1990), creator of the FDH, highlights a number of characteristics in which SLA is distinguished from L1 acquisition (see Table 2.2.):

1 lack of success
2 general failure
3 variation in success, course, and strategy
4 variation in goals
5 correlation of age and proficiency
6 fossilization
7 indeterminate intuitions (e.g. grammaticality judgments)
8 importance of instruction (e.g. quality of teaching)
9 negative evidence
10 role of affective factors

Based on these ten characteristics, try to formulate claims referring to the differences between L1A and SLA.

Table 2.2 Differences between L1A and SLA

1) lack of success 2) general failure 3) variation in success, course, and strategy	The success of SLA is not guaranteed, children and adults differ in the degree of attainment and L2 learners who will pass for native speakers will be rare cases (Slabakova 2009: 156).
4) variation in goals	L1 and L2 learners have different motivations.
5) correlation of age and proficiency 6) fossilization (see definition)	The higher the age effects, the lower the native-like acquisition. Fossilization is common only for SLA.
7) indeterminate intuitions	L2 learners have intuitions about grammaticality due to the variety of strategies they employ.
8) importance of instruction 9) negative evidence	The importance of instruction and practice for SLA may be due to the necessity of correction and negative evidence for learning (Slabakova 2009: 156).
10) role of affective factors	Affective factors play a role in SLA, but not in L1A.

The definition of fossilization, given by Han (2013), takes into account the innateness and the external manifestation of the phenomena. 'Fossilization' refers to the cognitive processes/mechanisms that produce permanently stabilized IL forms (fossilization is a process); it involves those stabilized IL forms that remain in L2 learners' speech and/or writing over time without any difference to the input to which the learner is exposed and to what the learner does with that input.

Fundamental Similarities Hypothesis

The Fundamental Similarities Hypothesis (FSH; Robinson, 1996, 1997) describes only the process of L2 acquisition by adults. As noted above, the FDH states that the various outcomes in success by adults are due to their different abilities to employ problem solving skills. The FSH, however, sees all adult SLA as fundamentally similar. It ascribes these similarities to the individual differences in cognitive abilities that adult learners bring to the task of processing L2 input. These differences are related to factors such as 'noticing' (see below) and higher-level awareness of the target language input. FSH does not differentiate between conscious versus unconscious acquisition and their possible outcomes: explicit versus implicit knowledge.

Children automatically acquire complex knowledge of the structures of their L1 through meaningful engagement, exposure to input and the assistance of their innate mechanisms. However, they cannot describe that knowledge. If you ask a child to tell you how the plurals of nouns are formed (explicit knowledge), he or she will not be able to do so. But, if you ask the child '*I have one banana and you have another banana. If I give you mine, what have you got?*' the child will be able to respond '*two bananas*' (implicit knowledge). The acquisition of L1 grammar is implicit and no explicit instruction is needed. In the case of SLA, adults receive formal instruction and tend to engage more with explicit learning.

According to FSH, learners' general cognitive abilities are applied to learning (which results from exposure to input in any condition) and they contribute to focal attention allocation, 'noticing' and rehearsal in memory. Attention, and awareness at the level of 'noticing' (Schmidt 1990, 2001) are necessary (but not sufficient) for subsequent L2 learning. The FSH is compatible with Schmidt's 'noticing' hypothesis, which claims awareness is necessary for L2 learning, but it is not compatible with Krashen's claims about unconscious L2 acquisition (see Chapter 1). The FSH argues that in adulthood there is no evidence for dissociation between unconscious and conscious learning (DeKeyser, 2015).

The FDH was reformulated by Bley-Vroman in 2009, when he made the case that what was not working well enough in SLA is the core system of the grammar. The reformulation of the FDH is complementary to Clahsen and Felser's (2006) Shallow Structure Hypothesis and Ullman's (2001) Declarative/Procedural Model of SLA. The Shallow Structure Hypothesis (SSH) states that during real-time language comprehension, L2 learners (regardless of their proficiency levels and language typology) can construct only shallow structure representations, relying almost exclusively on lexical and semantic information, because they lack sensitivity to syntactic cues in ambiguity resolution. In his Declarative/Procedural Model of SLA, Ullman (2001) suggests that adult and less proficient language learners rely heavily on declarative memory, even when processing regular inflections of words (e.g. plural *-s* or past simple *-ed*), while L1 learners rely on procedural memory. Procedural memory 'stores' knowledge that can be used without conscious reflection, such as the rules of one's native language (knowing how) while the declarative memory 'stores' facts, knowledge and experiences that can be consciously recalled (knowing what). In the L1, words (part of the mental lexicon) are stored and processed in declarative memory and mental grammar is stored and processed in procedural memory. In SLA, evidence indicates that both words and mental grammar are supported by declarative memory systems. According to Ullman (2001), L2 late learners have an attenuated procedural memory (age-related), which is why chunks (*walk+ed*) are memorized as such in their declarative memory.

If L2 late learners have attenuated procedural memory (and if it is age-related) and if their declarative memory is responsible for accessing the mental lexicon and grammar, what implications for teaching late less-proficient learners can you think of?

Implication 1:

Implication 2:

With regard to the implications for teaching and the application of Ullman's model, it implies that late and less proficient L2 learners will need both more frequent input and meaningful practice, which will affect the procedural system.

The role of the brain

Language is unique to the human brain, which has three main parts: the cortex (which regulates cognition); limbic system (which carries the emotional functions); and the brainstem. Two regions are related to language functions: the frontal lobe's language-sensitive region (Broca's area) and the temporal lobe's language-sensitive region (Wernicke's area). The human brain is designed to accommodate new experiences. Everything is stored in the brain's networks in multiple ways. Language is stored as sensory messages that are registered by the thalamus and relayed to the limbic system as well as the cortex. As we have learned, the process of SLA is a complex puzzle that a variety of theories attempts to resolve, but children manage to accomplish it with relative ease. What makes the human mind so special that it allows a young child to understand words and induce meaning and later to begin to use those words? How do humans discover forms and meanings? The science that investigates the role of the brain's functions in comprehending, producing and storing language data is called 'neurolinguistics'. Neurolinguists study brain activity and employ brain-imaging techniques that examine language processing, including electroencephalography (EEG)/event-related potentials (ERPs), magnetoencephalography (MEG), functional magnetic resonance imaging (fMRI) and near-infrared spectroscopy (NIRS).

Based on research findings regarding phonetic perception by infants, a number of explanations have been given about how computational, cognitive and social skills combine to form an extremely powerful learning mechanism that is different from Skinner's conditioning and reinforcement model of learning, but rather complex and multi-modal, having its roots in heightened attention (Kuhl 2010). Neurolinguists have compared the activity of the brain by L1 and L2 learners, bilingual and multilingual individuals. Their general findings suggest that some brain areas are shaped by early exposure to the L1, and are not necessarily activated by the processing of a second language to which participants have been exposed later in life, i.e. showing that L2s in late bilinguals (later acquisition in adulthood) are spatially separated from L1s (Perani *et al.* 1996, 1998). However, when acquired during the early language acquisition stage of development ('early' bilingual subjects), native and second languages tend to be represented in common frontal cortical areas (Kim *et al.* 1997).

Some parts of the brain may be necessary to process specific languages.

Do you think that this is a plausible explanation for the localization of the different languages in the brain? Why (not)?

Although neurolinguistic studies have managed to show that specific parts of the brain are activated when processing specific languages, this cannot be taken as a solid proof of the localization of the specific languages under question. Those brain regions/locations might be simply a connector between the other sub-systems stored in different regions of the brain. Neurolinguistics research has shown that language processing is spread over various parts of the brain (Stowe, Haverkort and Zwarts 2005), and related studies on multilingual individuals have focused on this question: to what extent is the processing of an L3 in the brain different from that of the L1 or L2? Based on a thorough review of the literature, Kees De Bot and Carol Jaensch (2015: 8) have concluded that there are no clear indications of multilingual individuals having different characteristics to bilinguals when it comes to aphasia and that the processing or decline of the L3 is not different from that of an L2. However, no hard conclusions can be drawn since numbers are small and assessment of skills in multiple languages is still rare. Similarly, though the number of neuroimaging data on multilingual subjects is small, those that do exist show no indications that the L3 is processed differently from the L2 (De Bot and Jaensch 2015).

Neurolinguists have also researched the effects of age on brain activity. Findings show that in both late and early bilingual subjects, Wernicke's area shows effectively little or no separation of activity based on the age of language acquisition. However, when comparing infants and young children with adults, neurolinguistic studies show that younger learners have the edge over adults, despite adults' cognitive superiority. Neurolinguists support the view that language is an example of a 'critical' or 'sensitive' period in neurobiology.

> Do you believe in a critical period beyond which individuals cannot acquire a language to a native-like level? Why (not)?

The 'best' age for learning a second language

As we have seen in the discussions about the differences between L1 acquisition and SLA (through the prism of the Fundamental Difference Hypothesis as well as according to neurolinguists), age has been cited as a contributory factor to success in language acquisition and this is upheld in the Critical Period Hypothesis (CPH). The origin of the CPH dates back to the 1960s and is linked to the field of biology. In the late 1950s and 60s, the Canadian brain surgeons Penfield and Roberts (1959) were the first to propose the idea that there is not only a critical period for L1 acquisition but also a biological constraint in human language learning. They based their hypothesis on their observations of the language behaviour of aphasics. One of their findings was that the brain was able to transfer speech functions from the damaged hemisphere to the undamaged one depending on the age (pre- or post-pubertal) of the aphasics: pre-adolescent aphasics were able to recover their speech without difficulty, while those who were past puberty were unable to do so. The expansion of the CPH to its application in the field of first language acquisition emerged through the work of Lenneberg, who in 1967 proposed that complete language acquisition must occur within a certain age range. There is evidence for incomplete first language acquisition for children exposed to linguistic training after the passage of the Critical Period who do not reach native-likeness. A well-known case of this type is Genie, who after suffering severe abuse and total isolation between the ages of one and a half to thirteen, was found to be without any language ability. Although she underwent intensive language intervention after she was found, her acquisition stopped at a level similar to that of a two-year-old child (Curtiss 1977). Curtiss suggested that the passage of the CP prevented Genie from employing language-specific learning and processing mechanisms.

Scholars are yet to reach a definitive conclusion about the existence of a Critical Period for SLA, and research on this issue is focused on the following three questions:

1 Are young language-learners 'better' at learning a second language?
2 Can late learners achieve native-like L2 proficiency?
3 If there is a cut-off point age, when is it?

Guess the answers of these three questions!

Answer to Question 1:

Answer to Question 2:

Answer to Question 3:

CPH studies fall into two opposite camps, and either support the theory or challenge it. Those scholars believing in a Critical Period for SLA take as their sole explanation the fact that there is a variation in success among L2 learners in comparison to L1 learners in the way they acquire and use the formal properties of the target language. Moreover, L2 learners differ from native speakers across a variety of language domains and measures. Studies, such as those conducted by Johnson and Newport (1989) as well as Coppieters (1987), suggest that even very advanced and near-native-like L2 learners did not perform within the same range as native speakers. These findings imply that post-Critical Period learners do not have an access to the UG and they employ different learning mechanisms than children and that the learning processes differ.

> Think of possible arguments about why the CPH should/could be rejected.
>
> Argument 1:
>
> Argument 2:
>
> Argument 3:

Marinova-Todd *et al.* (2000) pointed out three main misconceptions about age in the argument of those supporting the CPH: misinterpretation, misattribution and misemphasis:

1 misinterpretation of observations: the observation that 'children learn languages quickly, effortlessly and are like sponges, absorbing everything from the input' is false. There is evidence showing that children learn new languages slowly and painstakingly – indeed more slowly and with more effort than adolescents or adults.

2 misattribution of conclusions about the brain: the exact nature of connections between the brain's functioning and particular language performances/proficiencies cannot be guessed exactly from the data currently available.

3 misemphasis on failure: not focusing on the reasons why some post-critical period learners end up with lower than native-like levels of proficiency leads to missing important conditions for learning and teaching foreign languages. Those who do not pass for native-level

speakers are also those adult learners who at the same time fail to engage in various learning conditions, do not have sufficient motivation, and fail to commit the necessary time or energy, and who lack appropriate support in the learning process.

A number of empirical studies challenge and reject the CPH, stating that adult learners *do* have an access to the UG and employ the same learning mechanisms as children. These scholars use a variety of measures to test advanced speakers and show that there are indeed non-natives who have obtained native-like abilities (see, for example, Bialystok 1997; Birdsong 1992; Birdsong and Molis 2001; White and Genesee 1996). CPH data has also been re-analyzed to show that a different interpretation of the current data is possible. Here are some examples of studies that challenge the CPH across a variety of fronts, such as pronunciation, morphology and syntax.

CPH and pronunciation

Some studies (Bongaerts *et al.* 1997, Nikolov 2000) suggest that adults are, in fact, capable of attaining a native-like accent. Nikolov's study is interesting as it features thirty-three post-critical period language learners aged twenty to seventy. Twenty of these had different first languages and they were learning Hungarian as L2. Thirteen were L1 Hungarians learning English as L2. As judged by three groups of native speakers, Nikolov found out that six of the learners of L2 Hungarian and five of the learners of L2 English were generally and/or often mistaken for native speakers. Based on these findings, she concludes that any strong version of the CPH is questionable.

CPH and morphosyntax

White and Genesee's (1996) and Birdsong and Molis's (2001) studies both demonstrate the ability of adult second-language learners to achieve native-like proficiency as measured mainly by grammatical judgment tests. White and Genesee (1996) tested eighty-nine speakers of English as a second language, using a grammaticality judgment task, a question formation task and an interview task in which they were evaluated on their performance in terms of pronunciation, morphosyntax, fluency, choice of vocabulary and overall similarity to native speakers. Several subjects demonstrated an ability to achieve near-native levels of competence despite their age at first exposure (post-critical period), but White and Genesee also found that in terms of accuracy and speed, the performance of the near-native speakers was actually indistinguishable from that of the native speakers on both the grammaticality judgment tests, as well as on the written production task.

The extension of the CPH on areas other than accent opened up the possibility that different aspects of language may develop at different rates leading to differences in their criticality/sensitiveness. Oyama (1976) posits a tempered version of the CPH in which 'critical' is replaced by 'sensitive'. Another elaboration of the CPH is the existence of multiple critical/sensitive periods. For instance, late beginners can acquire other language 'components' more effectively than L2 phonology (Oyama 1976, Johnson and Newport 1989). In the SLA literature, varying ends of the offset have been set for subparts of language. Bialystok and Hakuta (1994) and Flege (1999) have found a linear decline in eventual outcome in tandem with increasing age of onset. In this vein, a number of positions have questioned the validity of a 'turning-point age', arguing that the effect of age on ultimate attainment (i.e. the degree to which L2 learners can develop native-like competence across different language domains) is not necessarily linked to any specific age span, but is rather successive over the entire lifespan.

If age alone as a factor is not sufficient to explain the differences in SLA by children and adults, what other contributory factors can you think of?

Different success rates and paths

The concept of ultimate attainment clearly is linked to differential success rates and paths across different L2 learners. Birdsong and Paik (2008) define the term 'ultimate attainment' (UA) as 'the outcome of L2A, irrespective of whether this outcome is similar to or different from nativelikeness' (Birdsong and Paik 2008: 424). The data gathered from ultimate attainment studies contributes a great deal to SLA theory, because it offers valuable findings about SLA limits. Ultimate attainment studies tackle many issues such as the question whether differences in final states imply differences in learning procedures. The following quotation illustrates best the potential of ultimate attainment state for the learning process:

Neither data relating to the pace of acquisition (e.g., numbers of contact hours required to reach a proficiency criterion) nor data relating to stages or developmental sequences in L2A speak directly to the acquisitional potential the L2 learner.

Birdsong and Paik 2008: 425

Thus, only data about upper limits of UA can reveal the constraints on learning. End-state data gives the SLA research community a sense of the range of final outcomes in SLA.

There are qualitative individual variations between learners as they display unequal states of interlanguage competence and varying distances towards that target end-state. Some aspects of language-learning seem to pose difficulties for particular individuals but not for others. The concept of fossilization may be taken here as an evidence showing that for a given learner part of his/her interlanguage system may fossilize and part of it may not. Such existence of intra-learner variation shows differential ultimate attainments within an individual learner's system where particular subsystems successfully reach the end-state and others do not.

A major focus of debate in the SLA field revolves around the cause for differential success. A variety of factors for the critical period effects have been operationalized in the CPH literature (see Table 2.3): motivational;

Table 2.3 Factors for the critical period effects

Type of factor	Study	Reason
Neurophysiological	Penfield and Roberts (1959)	Loss of cerebral plasticity
	Lenneberg (1967)	Lateralization
Cognitive	Clahsen and Muysken (1986)	Loss of access to Universal
	Bley-Vroman (1990)	Grammar
	Tsimpli and Roussou (1991)	Loss of access to parts of
	Hawkins and Chan (1997)	Universal Grammar
	DeKeyser (2000)	Decline in implicit learning
	Paradis (2004)	
	Newport (1990)	Rising complexity of analytical ability in adults
Affective-motivational	Krashen (1985)	Blocking effects of 'affective filter'
	Schumann (1978)	Increase in social and psychological distance
	Bialystok and Hakuta (1999)	Changes in psychosocial factors (simplified input, motivation, schooling)

emotional (such as psychological distance to the target-language community); and environmental (such as amount and type of L2 input).

With very few exceptions, such as DeKeyser and Larson-Hall (2005), the L2 learning context has not been included as an important factor in the discussion of the variations in CPH outcomes, and findings from second language learning in naturalistic contexts have been generalized to foreign languages in instructed contexts (Muñoz 2006: 6).

The amount and quality of input (exposure) to the target language is far more limited than in naturalistic environment. Thus, the offset and onset of any possible Critical Period should be questioned and analysed reasonably, because no identical correlations can be drawn between the two different processes of Foreign Language Learning (FLL) and SLA. The interactional processes in both contexts differ. For instance, a period of five years of natural exposure to a L2 would involve much more exposure in most cases than five years of formal L2 instruction, where the L2 is taught as just one school subject among many. The degree of strength and type of motivation of the individuals in both contexts may differ as well. Therefore, a critical examination of any application of the CPH in the FLL context is needed. A wealth of research studies were conducted on the effects of age on naturalistic second language acquisition, but very few studies have investigated these effects in formal learning situations and in combination, in which amount of exposure, offset and onset, amount of input and motivation, quality of input, type, quality and amount of instruction, aptitude, among many other factors, are taken into consideration.

SLA extended: third language acquisition

The spread of migration and the importance of languages in societies, business contexts and intercultural encounters has led to an increased interest in the topic of multilingualism. Due to the 'increasing movement of people (. . .) bilingualism and /or multilingualism have become the norm of many societies rather than being an exceptional phenomenon' (Şimşek 2006: 19).

The large body of studies on how L2s are acquired does not offer any insights into what goes beyond L2. SLA has been taken as an umbrella term for the acquisition processes of foreign languages beyond the acquisition of the first one. Similar terminological problems exist with the distinctions between the terms 'bilingualism' and 'multilingualism'. Some scholars have considered every individual who speaks two or more languages to be bilingual. The opposite is also true, and there are scholars who would describe even such individuals who only speak two languages (their first one and one foreign/second language) as 'multilingual'.

Even numerological numbering, such as L3, L4 and so forth has caused confusion in the field, as some label languages simply by the chronological order of acquisition without taking into consideration the proficiency in those languages. Others put under the label of L3 all other languages acquired subsequently. Besides these, there is the problem of common misunderstandings to the meaning of the term 'multilingual', very often used to describe a bilingual person who has acquired another language. More about this problematic elaboration can be found in the monograph by Gessica De Angelis (De Angelis 2007). Accounts such as those on multicompetence (Cook 2003) and multilingual competence seem not to be taken into consideration when designing language curricula in schools.

The construct of multilingual competence is very vague, undefined and difficult to describe. But what is known is that multilingual speakers possess a heightened language awareness as well as competences that help them to handle various communicative situations and to adjust their linguistic codes and communication styles to new contexts and situations. In this sense, it seems that we must place a great importance on the concept of multilingual competence, as it cannot be compared to that of a speaker learning a first foreign language. In the case of acquiring a second foreign language, we are dealing with an individual who faces the task with a greater confidence, is more experienced as a language learner and capable of handling communicative situations in a foreign language – the learner of a first foreign language has to start from scratch and work through the acquisition process.

Another elaboration of the qualitative and quantitative differences between bilingualism and multilingualism in terms of processing can be found in de Bot and Jaensch (2015). Based on a review of a large body of research, they conclude that from traditional linguistic and psycholinguistic perspectives there are grounds to differentiate monolingual, bilingual and multilingual processing. Kees de Bot has proposed the Dynamic System Theory (DST) for multilingualism. According to the DST, multilingualism is not a state, but a process. DST sees languages, dialects, registers and styles as tools for communication and as cognitive systems. They change as a result of external influences from the environment and internal reorganization of the system/s, i.e. the process is prone to growth and decline constantly and there is no end-state in language development. Language development is characterized by changes that are due to the learning of elements of a new language, which then also bring about changes to the rest of the language system and the other languages that that multilingual system consists of. According to the DST, it seems that when studying multilingualism, it only makes sense to analyze and study changes in all the multilingual system's languages longitudinally.

In recent years a couple of advancements, either in the form of overtaking the identical model of bilingualism for the separate linguistic subsystem or its adaptation, have been put forward. In regard to speech production, models of bilingual speech production have been taken as sufficiently adequate to account for multilingual speech production also (de Bot 1992; Green 1986; Grosjean 1992). In what follows we give a very short illustration of Green's activation/inhibition model. Based on data from studies on code-switching and bilingual aphasia, Green concludes that the languages acquired by bilinguals show different levels of activation. When a bilingual person speaks, a degree of selection takes place, and one of the languages he or she has acquired will be the active one (the one which participates in the speech processor) and the other one will be dormant, stored in the long-term memory and not really active in the speech process itself. The active language controls the output. A decade later, Green developed the inhibitory model to emphasize multiple levels of control.

The area of studying the mental lexicon is more complex and a variety of factors play a role in the organization of the multilingual lexicon as well as the proficiency in the different languages. Time is one of these factors, but others that influence the mental lexicon in general are prior language knowledge, the relations between the languages spoken (cross-linguistic influences), language distance or (psycho-)typology, recency of use, length of residence and exposure, order of acquisition, context etc. Based on this repertoire of influential issues, differences seem to be expected. Hence, it is claimed that multilingual individuals are learners and speakers are different than L2 learners and, consequently they should be treated as such. A multilingual speaker is then an individual who has multiple sources to refer to and who possesses a competence in which languages are inter-connected. In line with this, Cenoz and Gorter (2011: 339) have proposed a holistic approach to multilingual education which 'takes into account all of the languages in the learner's repertoire'. However, there is still lack of practical applications for how such an approach may be implemented in classroom settings. For example, 'English as a foreign language' is often treated as a separate school subject in Europe not related to the development of multilingual competence. Concrete pedagogical implications regarding multilingualism are still missing, though first attempts have been made (Jessner 2013; Vetter 2012).

Real-world applications

Based on the theoretical positions and views presented in this chapter, there are four main aspects which have real world applications:

1 the role of the language instructor within the UG theory;

2 useful aspects for language instructors based on Ullman's model;

3 useful aspects for language instructors based on the Processability Theory;

4 how language instructors should approach the topic of 'differences'.

In this section, we approach each of these four issues and illustrate real-world applications. We end this section with two practical and challenging tasks.

The role of the language instructor within the UG theory

Within the UG theory, the role of the teacher is limited to structuring the learning path through a presentation of good linguistic data which learners react to and work with in order to develop the correct mental representations of the target language. Hence, the teacher provides learners with useful linguistic input, which can be manipulated if needed. This input interacts with the internal/innate grammar of learners and that input is the key needed for learners to reset their internal parameters which constrain the learning. The role of the teacher is restricted to presenting the input useful for the required re-setting.

Useful aspects for language instructors based on Ullman's model

Ullman's declarative/procedural model offers valuable applications for teachers when considering the proficiency of the learners and the type of the input needed for meaningful practice to take place. In this regard, and as noted, his model claims that late and less proficient L2 learners will need more frequent input and meaningful practice affecting the procedural system.

Useful aspects for language instructors based on the Processability Theory

According to the Processability Theory, stages of acquisition can be neither skipped nor altered by instruction and instruction will be beneficial if it focuses on structures from the 'the next' stage (Pienemann 1998). This means that the teacher should provide input focusing on structure that a learner is close to acquiring. Instruction should be beneficial to acquisition as regards the rate of acquisition, the frequency of rule application and the different linguistic context in which the rule is applied. In accordance with this theory, teachers should be aware that not everything that is taught can necessarily be learned. Furthermore, teachers need to be able to differentiate between developmental and variational errors.

Activity

Dispute the following criticism expressed about the Processability Theory:	Your arguments:
It is difficult to determine what is to be taught when (Lightbown 1998: 179).	
There is a great variation of learners' developmental readiness within one classroom. Thus, it is difficult to teach according to the PT stages if you have to deal with 30 pupils.	
Communicative language teaching without 'later-acquired phenomena' (see developmental sequences and features in them) is not possible (Nunan 1994: 267).	

How should language instructors approach the topic of 'differences'?

Understanding the differences between adults and children is important for teachers, especially if they are aware of the drawbacks linked to some factors. For example, in naturalistic settings the amount and quality of input (exposure) to the target language is greater than in instructed settings. In addition, adults have far more developed analytic skills than younger learners. Understanding learners' individual differences will influence teachers' decisions about teaching methods or the type of materials they choose to work with. Knowledge about the qualitative individual variations in attaining competence in an L2, and realizing that learners display unequal states of interlanguage competence and varying distances towards that target end-state, helps teachers to understand learners' varying performances and support students on their way to successful acquisition. Teachers need to be familiar with learners' preferences, interests, motivations, personalities and repertoire of learning strategies in order to be able to develop effective pedagogical techniques and methods.

Activity

Think about the most appropriate teaching approach you could take when dealing with the following problems:

a) Output: 'This is Mary's book' (6th grade pupil, loves learning by doing, hates rules, very extrovert).
b) Almost all pupils in your class do not know how to form the past simple tense.
c) Pupils have problems with the articles in English: they can neither use them correctly, nor can they notice them.

a)
b)
c)

Where to find more about this topic

Birdsong, D., and Paik, J. (2008). Second language acquisition and ultimate attainment. In B. Spolsky and F. Hult (eds), *Handbook of Educational Linguistics* (pp. 424–436). Oxford: Blackwell.

Bley-Vroman, R. (2009). The evolving context of the Fundamental Difference Hypothesis. *Studies in Second Language Acquisition*, 31, 175–198.

Clahsen, H., and C. Felser (2006). How native-like is non-native language processing? *Trends in Cognitive Sciences,* 10 (12), 564–570.

De Angelis G. (2007) *Third or Additional Language Acquisition.* Clevedon: Multilingual Matters.

DeKeyser, R. (2015). Skill Acquisition Theory. In B. VanPatten and J. Williams (eds), *Theories in Second Language Acquisition* (2nd ed.; pp. 94–112). New York: Routledge.

Pienemann, M., and Lenzing, A. (2015). Processability theory. In B. VanPatten and J. Williams (eds), *Theories in Second Language Acquisition* (2nd ed.; pp.159–179). New York: Routledge.

Schwieter, J. W. (ed.) (2015). *The Cambridge Handbook of Bilingual Processing.* Cambridge: Cambridge University Press.

Ullman, M. (2001). The declarative/procedural model of lexicon and grammar. *Journal of Psycholinguistic Research*, 30, 37–69.

VanPatten, B., and Benati, A. (2010). *Key Terms in Second Language Acquisition.* London: Continuum.

Vetter, E. (2012). Multilingualism pedagogy: building bridges between languages. In J. Hüttner, B. Schiftner, B. Mehlmauer, and S. Reichl (eds), *Theory and Practice in* EFL *Teacher Education. Bridging the Gap* (pp.228–246). Bristol: Multilingual Matters.

White, L. (2003). *Second Language Acquisition and Universal Grammar*. Cambridge: Cambridge University Press.

How learners process information in second language acquisition

3

Introduction

This chapter examines how individuals process information in SLA. Input is a key ingredient in SLA, but learners do not process all the input (intake) they are exposed to thanks to a number of linguistic and processing factors constraining the way learners process information and language.

As we will outline, the role of instruction in SLA is limited. This is due to a number of external (access to good input language) and internal factors (natural processes and universal properties of the target language).

The 'individual differences' discussed below refer to a number of personal characteristics that might affect human thinking and behaviour. However, these have not consistently been found to be a predictor of success in second language acquisition. In this chapter a brief overview of five individual differences (age, language aptitude, working memory, learning strategies and motivation) will be provided.

We do not learn everything we are taught

Language growth

Researchers and theorists view SLA as a largely implicit and unconscious process that is guided principally by the learner's interaction with L2 input.

Yet the debate about whether this is the case or whether it is, in some cases, the product of an interface between explicit and implicit knowledge has continued for some time (see Chapter 4 for a full discussion of this issue). From a processing perspective, what needs to be established is how L2 learners process linguistic information and how their ability develops over time (from this position some aspects of SLA are innate). From a skill acquisition perspective, what needs to be established is how people progress in learning a variety of language skills from initial to proficient levels.

There are three main positions about language growth:

1   the implicit-unconscious position (or 'non-interface position') argues that explicit learning about an L2 is possible, but this ability remains separate from the underlying competence in the L2 that the learners come to acquire (Krashen's Monitor Theory; Krashen 1982). This position is consistent with nativist perspectives drawn from theories on linguistic universals. Researchers working in the generative framework agree that SLA consists mainly of implicit processes and that explicit learning cannot transform into implicit learning. Emergentism supports the view that although L2 learners engage in explicit language learning, SLA is largely implicit and the vast majority of our cognitive processing is unconscious. Explicit knowledge does not become implicit knowledge through practice.

2   the 'strong interface position' argues that explicit L2 knowledge, attained through explicit learning, *can* become implicit L2 knowledge. This is generally achieved through practice in which learners deliberately focus their attention on L2 form as it encodes message-meaning and allows them to work towards understanding and internalization. SLA is viewed as a skill, and its acquisition as a linguistic system is assumed to be built up gradually through processes of attention, conscious awareness and practice. The Adaptive Control of Thought model (ACT) is the foundation of the skill theory that distinguishes between two types of knowledge: declarative and procedural. Acquisition begins with declarative knowledge (e.g. information about the language, rules) and slowly becomes proceduralized (acquired by performing a skill) through practice (Skill Acquisition Theory). McLaughlin (1987) sees acquisition as a continuing movement from controlled processing in short-term memory to automatic processing in long-term memory. For Anderson (1983), a cognitive stage (where knowledge is learned through analysis and observation) follows an associative stage (where learners work out how to perform a skill) and an autonomous stage (where the skill becomes increasingly automatic). DeKeyser (2015)

equates SLA to skill learning, arguing that it develops from controlled to automatic processing. Declarative knowledge involves acquisition of isolated facts and rules (e.g. knowing *that* a car can be driven); procedural knowledge, on the other hand, requires practice and involves processing of longer units and increasing automization (e.g. knowing *how* to drive a car).

3 the 'weak interface position' questions the extent to which explicit learning and explicit instruction might influence implicit learning, and has identified possible limitations for instruction. Supporters of this position assume that SLA is predominantly implicit, yet have also argued that the linguistic system can be built up through a number of instructional interventions that enable learners to notice and process crucial relationships of L2 form and meaning in the language input and eventually process these as form–meaning mappings.

The role of instruction in SLA

Does instruction make a difference? The answer is that we do not learn everything we are taught. Over the last fifty years scholars and practitioners have been debating whether instruction makes a difference in the acquisition of language properties such as morphology and syntax. Contemporary theories (VanPatten and Williams 2015) seem to suggest that there are two main positions on the role of instruction in second language acquisition (see also VanPatten and Benati 2015):

1 instruction does not make a difference;
2 instruction might be beneficial.

Instruction does not make a difference

As discussed in Chapter 1, the Monitor Theory (Krashen 1982, 2009) argues that instruction plays a limited role in second language acquisition. Krashen suggests that L2 learners acquire language mainly through exposure to comprehensible and meaning-bearing input. Learners internalize grammar by being exposed to samples of language in a specific communicative context. The Theory holds that acquisition of the grammatical system of another language is driven by the exposure to the input and not by the practising of grammatical rules, and also indicates that grammar instruction is constrained by the acquisition of some linguistic features in a fixed and predicted order. Morphological features such as the progressive -*ing* in English is acquired (regardless of the learner's L1) before the regular past tense -*ed*, or irregular past tense forms, which are acquired before the third-person singular -*s*. Instruction is therefore constrained by universal and predictable orders of acquisition.

The Universal Grammar Theory (White 2003, 2015) views language as an abstract and complex system. Although many aspects of language are acquired by interaction with input (e.g. syntax, morphology and lexicon), one exception is those aspects of language that are universal and built in prior to exposure to the input language. All humans have universal features of language which constraint the acquisition of grammar. For example, sentences have underlying hierarchical structure consisting of phrases (e.g. noun phrase, verb phrase) which require a 'head' and a 'complement'. This information is built into L2 learners' internal systems and learners make use of the input to process any possible variations in the target language. Instruction has no effect on this subconscious knowledge. Learners create an abstract system (mental representation) similar to that of L1 learners (see Chapter 4). For example, sentences have an underlying hierarchical structure consisting of phrases, and these phrases require a head and a complement:

- noun phrase (NP) = noun (head) + complement = Alessandro *is a professor*
- verb phrase (VP) = verb (head) + complement = *teaches Italian*
- prepositional phrase (PP) = preposition (head) + complement = *at the University of Greenwich*

Learners do not need input to know that languages are hierarchical and consist of phrases. This comes automatically because such information is 'built' in (implicit) to the universal properties of languages. This representation bears little to no resemblance to what is traditionally taught and practised (grammatical rules). Mental representation builds up over time due to consistent and constant exposure to input data. It needs input to know whether there are variations between two languages. For example, English is head initial (VP) and Japanese is head final (VP). In order for learners of English to build a system with head final if they learn Japanese, they need input to be able to interact mentally with universal properties.

The Processability Theory (Pienemann 1998; Pienemann and Lenzing 2015) argues that L2 learners acquire single structures (i.e. negation, question formation) through predictable stages. The theory argues that instruction is constrained by these developmental stages, and L2 learners follow a very rigid route when they acquire grammatical structures. The main implication of this view is that the role of instruction is therefore limited by L2 learners' readiness to acquire a particular structure, and indeed might be detrimental to acquisition if it does not consider learners' current developmental stage. Instruction must consider learners' psycholinguistic readiness if it is going to be effective. Developmental sequences in L2 learners' acquisition of tense and aspect, both of which involve the acquisition of morphological features, have been studied intensively in SLA in recent years. Research into the acquisition of tense and aspect lend strong support to the existence of developmental patterns in L2 acquisition, and it seems that L2 learners create linguistic systems in a systematic and dynamic way that are ostensibly little affected by external forces such as instruction and correction.

Instruction might be beneficial

The Input Processing Theory (VanPatten 2004, 2015) refers to how learners initially perceive formal features of language input, and the strategies or mechanisms that might guide learners in processing these. Learners seem to process input for meaning (words) before they process it for form (grammatical features), and typically parse sentences by assigning subject or agent status to the first noun or pronoun they encounter. These default strategies cause a delay in the acquisition of formal properties of the target language. According to this theory, instruction is effective and beneficial if it manipulates input in such a way that learners process grammar more efficiently and accurately. The pedagogical model derived from this theory is called the Processing Instruction. According to this model, learners should be exposed to meaningful input that contains many instances of the same grammatical meaning–form relationship (e.g. the verb ending –ed encodes a past event). Grammar instruction should be designed to circumvent default processing strategies and replace them with appropriate ones.

The Skill-Learning Theory (DeKeyser 2015) views SLA as a process which entails going from controlled mode (declarative knowledge) to automatic mode (procedural knowledge) through repeated practice. The theory suggests that learners need to be taught explicitly and need to practise the various grammatical features and skills until they are well established (fluency). Instruction is beneficial when it helps explicit knowledge to become proceduralized.

For the proponents of emergentism and usage-based Theories (Ellis and Wulff 2015), SLA is mainly implicit and frequency in the input language plays a key role. Language and its properties emerge over time and are the result of cognitive mechanisms interacting with input. Although the role of instruction is limited and it is not always effective, it can have a facilitative role in developing 'noticing' of target forms which might not be salient in the input language.

According to the Interaction Hypothesis (Gass and Mackey 2015), comprehensible input alone might not be sufficient for L2 learners to develop native-like grammatical competence. Students should therefore be involved in meaningful learning tasks where they have opportunities to communicate and negotiate meaning. Instruction might be beneficial if it is provided by enhancing the input through the use of different techniques (e.g. input enhancement, textual enhancement), and could have a facilitative role in helping learners pay attention to the formal properties of a targeted language without the need of metalinguistic discussion.

Sociocultural Theory (Lantolf, Thorne and Poehner 2015) regards instruction as crucial to L2 development in the classroom and – as outlined in Chapter 1 – should be geared to the Zone of Proximal Development (ZPD) that is beyond the learners' actual development level. The theory suggests that during instruction (both metalinguistic and explicit), learners develop an awareness of the structure and function of language by using it socially. The environment provides the context and assists in the understanding of grammatical properties of the language.

From this review of contemporary theories on the role of instruction in SLA we can draw the following conclusions:

- instruction does not alter the route of acquisition (i.e., acquisition orders and developmental sequences);
- instruction may have some beneficial effects (see below);
- instruction can manipulate input and facilitates language processing;
- instruction might be able to foster explicit and implicit interfaces;
- instruction can foster learners' attention to language forms in the course of meaningful task interaction.

What are the implications of these findings for grammar instruction?

Name three main real-world implications for teaching.

1

2

3

Not all input can be comprehended and acquired at once

The input processing perspective

Language acquisition does not occur (even if input of the right quantity and quality is given) without being internalized by the learners and becoming part of their interlanguage system. SLA takes place when learners understand input that contains grammatical forms that are at a higher level than the current state of their interlanguage. However, we know that only part of the language input learners are exposed to is actually being processed (intake) and accommodated into the developing system. Changing the way L2 learners process input and enriching their intake might therefore have an effect on the quality and the quantity of input fed into the developing system. This should subsequently have an impact on how learners access the new language in the input to produce the L2 (see Chapter 4 for a discussion around the role of output and the processing strategies required by learners to access the system for speech-production purposes). Overall, interpretation of the input language involves processing for meaning and processing for competence change. In the first scenario, L2 learners are exposed to the input and might process it for meaning in order to cope with communication demands. In the second scenario, L2 learners process input for acquisition as input might trigger a change in their interlanguage and they may be able to convert the input into intake.

Input is a necessary and vital factor for the acquisition of a L2 and provides the primary linguistic data for the creation of an implicit unconscious linguistic system: 'No model of second language acquisition does not avail itself of input in trying to explain how learners can create second language grammars' Gass (1997: 1). As noted, however, not all input becomes intake and learners are not always able to store the grammatical information about the target language into their developing system. Some L2 learners may need further input.

From an input-processing perspective, when learners process language input and comprehend the message, a form–meaning connection is made. Developing the ability in L2 learners to map one form to one meaning is essential for acquisition. Input gets 'hanged' when L2 learners attend to too many stimuli, and therefore they filter the information, using internal strategies to cope with the amount of information they receive. The input-processing capacity of L2 learners is limited, however, and their internal processors might not detect all the linguistic data available. One of the key questions addressed in SLA research is: what causes certain stimuli in the input to be detected and not others? When learners process input, they filter the input, which is reduced and modified into a new entity called intake. As we know, only part of the input L2 learners receive is processed and becomes intake, and this is due primarily to processing limitations, as our working memory does not have enough capacity to do much more than process content words. VanPatten (2015) has identified a series of processing strategies/ principles used by L2 learners when they process and filter linguistic data at input level, and which allow learners to selectively attend to incoming stimuli without being overloaded with information. The two main principles in VanPatten's input processing theory are:

1 Principle 1 (P1). The Primacy of Meaning Principle. Learners process input for meaning before they process it for form.
2 Principle 2 (P2). The First Noun Principle. Learners tend to process the first noun or pronoun they encounter in a sentence as the subject / agent.

Principle 1

During input processing, L2 learners initially direct their attention towards the detection of content words to understand the main meaning of an utterance. Learners tend to focus their attention onto content words in order to understand the message of the input they are exposed to but in so doing they fail to process grammatical forms, and consequently are unable to make form–meaning connections. This is the case for forms which are redundant in the input, as occurs when, in a sentence or discourse, a grammatical form and a word encode the same semantic information. When this happens, L2 learners tend to process words before grammatical forms (in the sentence *'Yesterday I played tennis in the park'*, learners would process the temporal adverb first before the verbal inflection *-ed* as in *played*). A form–meaning mapping is achieved where L2 learners are be able connect a form with its meaning (in this particular order) in the input they receive (e.g. the morpheme *-ed* on the end of the verb in English refers to an event in the past).

Can you think of some examples of a form–meaning connection learners might have to make in the input they receive?

Principle 2

As discussed above, L2 learners also tend to process the first noun or pronoun they encounter in a sentence as the subject or agent (the First Noun Principle), a processing strategy that typically leads them to misinterpret the meaning of an utterance and delay acquisition. L2 learners must be able to determine, for example, which is the subject and which is the object in a sentence they hear or read (e.g. *'The police officer was killed by the robber'*).

Can you think of some examples of structure affected by the First Noun Principle?

The connectionist perspective

The Competition Model (MacWhinney 2001) emphasizes the concept that all linguistics performance requires the 'connecting' of language forms and functions. The forms are morphological inflections and word order patterns, while the functions are grammatical functions with specific semantic properties. The mapping of one form and one function is part of first language (L1) acquisition and according to the model SLA is about adjusting the existing mapping system in the L1 acquisition with the one appropriate in the second language. Input plays a key role in the model in terms of providing multiple cues for learners. Acquisition of appropriate form–meaning mappings is driven by a number of factors, most of which are related to the reliability of a particular cue. The following factors are the key indicators of cue reliability:

1 frequency. This factor relates to how often a form–meaning connection occurs in the input. If it is frequent, then the cue is strengthened and L2 learners can rely on it.

2 contrastive availability. This factor relates to the question of whether or not the cue has a contrastive effect. If it does not – as is the case of forms made redundant, for example – the cue will tell learners nothing about form–meaning mappings.

3 reliability. Some cues are more reliable than others in helping learners to make a correct interpretation. We will discuss this in Chapter 4.

Connectionist approaches (Ellis 2002) focus on the possible associations between stimuli and responses. Overall connectionism is based on the notion of the gradual emergence of interconnected networks of simple units. According to the Parallel Distributed Processing Approach, acquisition occurs in a network of connected units in the brain. Learners extract regularities from the input and associations are formed and eventually strengthened. The strength of the associations is determined by two main factors: the frequency of input; and the nature of feedback. For successful production and interpretation to take place, the connections must be activated simultaneously rather than sequentially.

The Modular Online Growth and Use of Language (MOGUL) is a processing framework proposed by Truscott and Sharwood Smith (2004). MOGUL integrates a UG perspective with a connectionist perspective

Figure 3.1 MOGUL memory stores, processors and interfaces

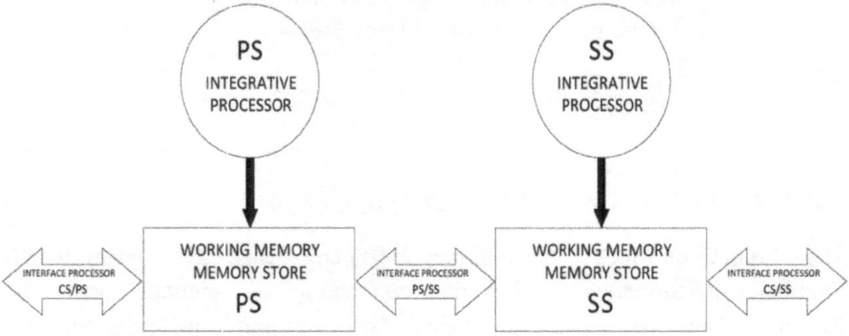

(known as the Competition Model) in order to explain language learning. MOGUL consists of three systems: phonological (PS); morphosyntactical (SS); and conceptual (CS).

Structures can work either in isolation or by communicating information with each other through the interfaces in a modular way (see Figure 3.1).

In this framework, the conceptual system operates at a conscious level, but the phonological system and morphosyntactical system do not.

Functional perspective

A functional approach views language as a means of communication. Functionalists emphasize the importance of communication as learners use languages to express a concept. Functionalism relates to the concept and role of forms and language functions, and to research into the acquisition of tense and aspect. This research addresses two questions:

1 how do we report whether something is past, present, or future?

2 how do people view and report events regardless of tense?

An aspectual difference refers to how people choose to report the event or what 'aspect' of the event they are reporting. A person can report any event as one that is in progress (such as '*Alessandro is watching TV*') or not (such as '*Alessandro watches TV all day*'). According to functionalists (Bardovi-Harlig 2000; Klein 2009), L2 learners might begin to express the function of temporality through adverbs (e.g., 'yesterday morning', 'today', 'last night', etc.).

Functionalists are interested in establishing: first, how the learners' expression of temporality changes over time; and second, what the interplay is between the various linguistic resources available to learners at any given point in time during acquisition.

Learners move through several different stages in their interplay among means of expression (expression of the past):

- the pragmatic stage (scaffolding), where learners use discourse. 'Scaffolding' is a term used to describe what happens in some interactions with both first and second language learners. While the non-native speaker (NNS) may produce limited and incomprehensible utterances, the native speaker (NS) is speaking in full sentences. It has been claimed that scaffolding can assist learners' development by providing the language needed for production.

- the lexical stage, where temporal adverbs are used to indicate time and to establish a time orientation.

- the morphological stage (where past morphology develops) to indicate a time relation. First learners rely on lexical items to express time and subsequently make use of verbal morphology when it becomes more reliable.

Despite these stages, the effects of instruction on interlanguage are constrained by the developmental acquisition stages (processability theory) even when learners have established means of expressing a given concept in interlanguage.

One of the main concepts among functionalists is that language is seen as the mapping of form and function. The question is how this mapping might influence our interlanguage development considering that meaning and function have a central role in SLA. Every linguistic device (structure, word or morpheme) has a functional load (communicative value) that depends on redundancy. Learners' interlanguage systems select form–meaning mappings on a one-to-one basis (mapping one form to one meaning). Evidence from input-processing studies (on accuracy and rate of processing-redundancy) supports this view.

Activity

Read the following study: Lee, J. F. (2002). The incidental acquisition of Spanish future tense morphology through reading a second language. *Studies in Second Language Acquisition*, 24, 55–80.

- Purpose
- Research questions
- Design
- Results
- Interpretation and significance
- Implications, limitations and further research

Interaction perspective

According to the Interaction Hypothesis, input can be distinguished as either interactional or non-interactional. Interactional input refers to input received during interaction where there is some kind of communicative exchange involving the learner and at least another person (e.g. a conversation, classroom discussions). L2 learners are able to negotiate meaning and make some conversational adjustments. This means that conversation and interaction make linguistic features salient to the learner and negotiation can facilitate acquisition. Non-interactional input refers to the kind of input that occurs in the context of non-reciprocal discourse and learners are not part of an interaction (e.g. announcements).

Conversational (Gass and Mackey 2015) interaction and negotiation can facilitate acquisition. Learners sometimes request clarifications or repetitions if they do not understand the input they receive. In the attempt to facilitate acquisition, one person can ask the other to modify his or her utterances or the person might modify his or her own sentences in order to be understood. In conversations involving NNSs, negotiations are frequent and typically include confirmation checks (e.g. *'did you say . . .?'*), comprehension checks (e.g. *'do you understand?'*) and clarification requests (e.g. *'what did you say?'*). Long (1996: 451) has suggested that 'negotiation for meaning, and especially negotiation work that triggers interaction adjustments by the NS (Native Speakers) or more competent interlocutor, facilitate acquisition because it connects input, internal learner capacities, particularly selective attention, and output in productive way'.

When it comes to language input, another distinction is made in instructed SLA research between positive and negative evidence. Positive evidence comprises the various utterances to which learners are exposed in the input as spoken and written language. Instructors can enhance the input to make learners notice particular forms for example (input enhancement). Negative evidence can be provided by the instructors through their feedback to L2 learners about the incorrectness of utterances, and can take several forms in conversational interaction, ranging from puzzled looks, confirmation checks and clarification requests to corrective recasts.

Attention and noticing are important parts of the acquisition of a second language and for many scholars (e.g. Schmidt 1995, 2001) they are necessary for learning to take place. SLA is driven by what L2 learners pay attention to and notice in the input. Attention can be defined as a cognitive process used by learners to selectively concentrate on one thing while ignoring other things. The three main concepts fundamental to attention are selection, capacity and effort.

Selection

Items that learners notice in input might be processed (noticing hypothesis). Schmidt (1990) has criticized Krashen's position, arguing that L2 learners require attention in order to successfully process forms in the input. Learners must pay attention to a form in the input and also notice it for that form to be processed and acquired. Schmidt's 'noticing hypothesis' suggests that noticing is necessary. A degree of awareness is also crucial if L2 learners are to incorporate the new language into their internal system. Therefore, for Schmidt, selection accompanied by noticing are the two main ingredients required for learners to acquire a second language. Overall, awareness has a limited role in SLA, as conscious learning has no or minimal effect on the ability of L2 learners to acquire and use a second language in spontaneous communication. Learners have a limited capacity for processing information and therefore select incoming stimuli from the several stimuli they are exposed to. One of the questions addressed by research into the role of attention as selection is to establish what and how language learners initially select and process in the input. L2 learners seem to select information early in the processing of the information. According to Schmidt's model, audio and visual information is first registered through the sensory system.

After detection, selected information enters into the working memory system. The basic assumption in this model is that L2 learners cannot process more than one form at a time. In addition to this, simultaneous attention to form and meaning is not possible.

Capacity

In second language acquisition, learners' limited attentional capacity makes it unlikely that they will be able to attend both to the message and formal features of a target language. Attention has been characterized as comprising three components:

1 alertness – learners' readiness to deal with incoming stimuli;
2 orientation – learners' ability to align attention to a stimulus;
3 detection – the selection of a particular piece of information.

'Detection' refers to the cognitive registration of the stimuli. It is the process responsible for selecting a specific piece of information, engaging it and registering it in the memory. Detection, rather than selection and noticing, is the key element for the derivation of intake from the L2 input. It is also a crucial component of attention, as it constitutes the process used by learners to register data in working memory. Robinson (2003), incorporating Schmidt

(2001) and Tomlin and Villa's model (2004), defined noticing as detection plus rehearsal in working memory before encoding in long-term memory. Robinson argued that both noticing and understanding are the result of rehearsal mechanisms, and the level of awareness is determined by the amount and rehearsal in the working memory. The 'capacity' of attention refers to the degree of attention allocated to the processing of information at any one time. Attention has a limited capacity as the brain's sensory system is presented with a large amount of stimuli at any time, and due to working memory constraints it is impossible to process them all. Both the number of stimuli and the amount of attention paid to each of them is therefore restricted. Two of the constructs often presented and examined in terms of capacity are the single resource pool and the multiple resource pool. The former argues that there is a single resource pool of attentional supply that L2 learners allocate to tasks. This resource varies in terms of an individual's arousal state and the demands of the task. Complex tasks would demand more attention than simpler and automatized tasks such that performing two tasks simultaneously is more demanding than one alone. The latter view expands the single resource pool and considers the possibility that two separate resource pools might be responsible for allocation of attention to different task demands. These resources include:

1 processing mechanisms (i.e. cognitive vs response processes);
2 processing modality (i.e. audio vs visual perception);
3 processing codes (i.e. spatial vs verbal activities).

Effort

The third concept related to the construct of attention refers to the learners' effort in processing information (Robinson 2003). It is assumed that sustained attention to a stimulus is essential for carrying out a task. The degree of effortful attention dedicated to a task depends on the capacity demands of that task: if demands are high, then more effortful attention is needed or the performance and processing might deteriorate. Those tasks demanding less attention would allow L2 learners to process more information and conduct a secondary task.

Individual differences

Research on SLA has investigated why some L2 learners are more successful than others despite the fact that the acquisition of a second language is clearly affected by natural and universal properties (orders and sequences of acquisition, universal grammar). Individual difference can be an explanation of language-acquisition variations: factors such as age, aptitude, working memory, learner strategies and motivation are shown below, and all of these have been considered as possible predictors of second language learning success.

- age is believed to be a key element in effective acquisition. It is based on the assumption that children are more successful than adults at learning a second language, but research findings are inconsistent.

- language aptitude is related to the broader concept of human abilities covering a variety of cognitive-based learner differences. A number of aptitude language tests (e.g. the Modern Language Aptitude Test (MLAT), CANAL-FT) have been developed over the years in order to predict the rate of progress and success under conditions such as motivation, opportunity to learn and quality of instruction. Here too, however, research has produced conflicting results.

- working memory plays a vital role in developing our ability to process linguistic data and is also essential for language processing (the ability to process symbols, store capacity and integrate information) in both comprehension and the production of language. A number of models have been developed to measure low- and high-span capacity in L2 learners and to establish whether they are conducive to efficient learning.

- individual learning strategies can also be seen as a factor influencing SLA. Skilled language-learners might make use of effective strategies to acquire a second language.

- motivation is crucial too in acquiring a new language, but might not provide us with an understanding of the processes involved therein.

Age

A great variety of views have been expressed on the correlation between age and ultimate attainment in SLA. The Critical Period Hypothesis (CPH) argues that there is a period of time during which humans display a heightened sensitivity to certain environmental stimuli and therefore it is easier for them to acquire a second language. According to this hypothesis, children are better second-language learners than adults because their brains are specifically organized to learn language whereas adults' are not. One of the key arguments in this hypothesis is that a child's brain is more flexible compared with that of an adult. Lenneberg (1967) asserted that language acquisition is mainly an innate process influenced by certain biological factors, which limits the critical period for acquisition of a language from two years of age to puberty. Lenneberg suggests that after lateralization (a process by which the two sides of the brain develop certain functions, normally completed at puberty), the brain loses plasticity, and it is therefore more difficult to acquire another language. Early exposure to a second language is therefore a potential advantage in acquiring it. The Sensitive Period Hypothesis also proposes a gradual deterioration in the process of language learning (Johnstone 2002) as we get older. The common view is that children have an advantage over adult learners in language-learning (Ellis 2008), and this view is supported by a number of studies comparing pre- and post-pubertal groups, which have indicated that the former are better at learning (Johnson and Newport 1991; Singleton 2001). Research on second language acquisition among immigrants has shown that the younger the child, the higher the probability of a native-like accent (Lightbown and Spada 2008). Children and adults have neurological, cognitive and psychological differences that come into play in SLA. Children tend to have fewer inhibitions than adults and are eager to actively participate in the social life around them. They do not have analytical skills and tend to process languages generally through sensory experience. Their language develops from exposure to the simplified and concrete while adult language learners struggle to master language structure. They do, however, have useful analytical skills, pragmatism and years of real-world experience and knowledge. These abilities and attributes might help them to perform language tasks with much greater complexity.

Researchers have found evidence that adults can also achieve high levels of ultimate success in the acquisition of a second language (Archibald 2005; DeKeyser 2000; Birdsong 2005, 2006; Singleton 2007). They argue that it is difficult to support the view that a critical period truly exists as there is contradictory evidence highlighting age as an indicator of successful language acquisition. As noted above, other factors such as the motivation to learn, access to input and opportunities for interaction are important determining variables that might affect the rate and success of second language acquisition. In examining the findings investigating the role of age in SLA, we might conclude that conflicting results and views have undermined the original CPH (see also Chapter 2).

At what age did you first learn a second language?

Name three individual factors which might have affected your learning.

1

2

3

Language Aptitude

Language aptitude is defined as a mixture of abilities that might facilitate language learning. Carroll (1981) has identified four main abilities:

1 phonemic coding ability. This is the learners' capacity to code sounds that can be retained. Considered a unique auditory component of foreign language aptitude, it is especially important in a language classroom which emphasizes spoken language.

2 grammatical sensitivity. This is the ability to recognize the functions of words in sentences. This component is relevant in language classes that emphasize an analytical approach to learning a foreign language.

3 inductive language learning ability. This is the capacity to infer and extrapolate rules to create new sentences. It is a kind of general memory, and learners seem to differ in the way they might apply and use their memory to the foreign language situation.

4 memory and learning. This is the capacity to form links in memory; like inductive learning ability, it may vary according to an individual's ability.

A number of aptitude tests to measure these abilities have been developed and the MLAT (Modern Language Aptitude Test) is probably the most influential currently available. It consists of five subtests:

1 a number learning test, to measure associative memory;

2 a phonetic script test, to measure phonemic coding capacity;

3 a spelling clues test, to measure high-speed language vocabulary and phonemic coding ability.

4 a words in sentences test, to measure grammatical sensitivity.

5 a paired associated test, to gauge associative memory.

The possible relation between aptitude and second language acquisition has received considerable attention in SLA theory and research. Skehan (1998) has argued that specific components of aptitude are related to stages of information processing, while Dörnyei and Skehan (2003) have attempted to make explicit links between stages of L2 processing and specific aptitude constructs (see Table 3.1 below).

They have suggested that it is possible for individual aptitude differences to have an effect on successful noticing and input processing. Individual phonetic coding ability and working-memory capacity might therefore influence the way learners acquire a second language. Robinson (2001) has challenged the concept of isolated aspects of aptitude and instead has developed a new concept, which involves what he called 'Aptitude Complexes' (aptitude for focus on form;

Table 3.1 Stages of L2 processing and their related aptitude constructs

Stages of L2 processing	Aptitude constructs
Input processing strategies	Attentional control, working memory
Noticing	Phonetic coding ability, working memory
Pattern identification	Phonetic coding ability, working memory grammatical sensitivity, inductive language learning ability
Pattern restructuring and manipulation	Inductive language learning ability
Pattern control	Automatization, integrative memory
Pattern integration	Chunking, retrieval memory

aptitude for incidental learning (oral and written); aptitude for explicit rule learning). In the Aptitude Complex Hypothesis, Robinson claims that learning draws on different combinations of cognitive abilities (aspects of aptitude) depending on the conditions of instructional exposure. He makes an explicit call for more research to investigate the extent to which various instructional treatments (e.g., processing instruction; input enhancement) may or may not be sensitive to individual differences within these aptitude complexes.

Working memory

Memory is the ability to encode, store and retrieve information. Three types of memory have been identified: sensory memory; short-term memory/ working memory; and long-term memory.

Sensory memory is responsible for receiving the information through different modalities. This information is subsequently processed and only a small proportion of it enters the short-term memory. Sensory memory and short-term memory are limited in their capacity to process and store information (Skehan 1998).

Short-term memory receives input from the sensory system and then transfers information to long-term memory which is capable of storing information for an extended period of time. Baddeley and Hitch (1994) renamed short-term memory as 'working memory'. It can be defined as 'the ability to mentally maintain information in an active and accessible state, while concurrently and selectively processing new information' (Conway *et al.* 2007: 3). A number of accounts have been put forward to describe the precise nature of working memory. However, the most prominent account is the model proposed by Baddeley (2003). According to this model, working memory consists of a limited capacity store and is supported by two systems: the phonological loop which is responsible for processing auditory information; and the visual-spatial sketchpad, which is responsible for processing visual information.

Long-term memory refers to a system for storing information so that it can be retrieved at a later stage. The storage capacity is extremely difficult to quantify and many attempts have been made over the years to do so. It appears that items in long-term memory might be stocked in associative networks (VanPatten 2003).

Working memory refers to the 'processing space in the mind/brain when a person holds and computes information' (VanPatten and Benati 2010: 167). It is, however, possible that information entered in the working memory does not enter into long-term memory for processing because some parts of the input are selected for further processing and other parts are suppressed at the perception stage (Schmidt 2001). As VanPatten and Benati (2010: 167) point out: 'there are multiple theories and models of working memory, but what they all have in common is the idea that working memory has a limited capacity. That is, a person can only process and store in working memory a limited amount of information before it must be disposed of so that the person can continue processing new incoming information.'

A range of empirical studies (Martin and Ellis 2012) within a cognitive and psycholinguistic account of language acquisition have been conducted to investigate the role of working memory in second language acquisition. Overall these studies have provided empirical support for the view that working memory plays a direct role in the acquisition of an L2 under certain conditions of exposure: processing capacity; input; and task demands.

Learning strategies

Learning strategies refer to the techniques, behaviours, actions and processes used by L2 learners to make language acquisition easier and faster. Language strategies can be described within a cognitive and dynamic view of language learning. In this view, learners process information from the input, organize it and relate it to what they already know, retain some of it, and eventually use the information in appropriate contexts. Three functional groups of learning strategies can be identified: cognitive; metacognitive; affective and social (O'Malley and Chamot 1990).

Meta-cognitive strategies refer to the following: planning (advance organizers, directed and selective attention, functional planning); monitoring (checking, verifying, or correcting comprehension and performance during language tasks); and evaluating the language task (checking the outcomes of the task once it has been completed.

Cognitive strategies involve the manipulation or transformation of the language to be learned. The term refers to activities such as repetition, translation, deduction, guessing meaning, auditory representation, inferencing, note-taking, and summarizing,

Social/affective strategies mainly involve the learner in communicative interaction with native speakers and non-native speakers, for instance, when collaborating with peers in problem-solving tasks.

Research on learning strategies (O'Malley and Chamot 1990) has provided the following insights:

- intermediate language learners tend to use more metacognitive strategies than beginners;
- those students at beginners' level tend to use cognitive strategies more than do intermediate-level students;
- overall, effective language learners, regardless of proficiency levels, use a variety of strategies, matching them to their own learning style and personality and also to the demands of the task in the context of cultural influences. Good learners find ways to tailor their use of strategies to their individual needs and requirements. They develop a combination of strategies that work for them.

Grenfell and Macaro (2007) suggest that the use of learning strategies remains an ambiguous field of enquiry and future research will need to investigate how learners combine strategies and why certain learners are able to do this more effectively than others.

Motivation

There are a number of definitions for this difference, which varies between individuals. Gardner defines motivation as: 'the combination of effort plus desire to achieve the goal of learning the language plus favourable attitudes towards learning the language' (Gardner 2001: 10). Others see motivation as a dynamic process showing a certain amount of changeability (Dörnyei 2006). In Gardner's socio-educational model, motivation to acquire a second language includes three main elements: the effort undertaken by the individual to learn a language; the willingness to achieve a goal; the enjoyment in the task of learning a second language. Dörnyei's definition states that 'Motivation theories attempt to explain nothing less than why people behave and think as they do, and human nature being as complex as it is, there are no simply cut-and-dried answers to be offered' (Dörnyei 2001: 2). Lightbown and Spada (2001: 33) identify motivation in second language acquisition as 'a complex phenomenon which can be defined in terms of two factors: learners' communicative needs and their attitudes towards the second language community'.

Motivation is considered important in SLA as it might have an influence on language achievement. There are two types of motivation that might affect learning a language: integrative and instrumental (Gardner 2001).

- integrative motivation means learning a language with the intention of participating in the culture of that language's people. It occurs when learners feel drawn to a certain group of people or culture.

- instrumental motivation suggests and implies that learners acquire the language in support of a purpose such as increasing occupational or business opportunities.

Intrinsic and extrinsic motivation is another distinction made by scholars (Ryan and Deci 2000) in the attempt to define motivation. Intrinsic motivation is the eagerness and interest to participate in certain activities – in this case learning a language – because of the benefits derived from acquiring new skills and gaining and processing new knowledge. In short, intrinsically motivated learners will enjoy learning a language. Extrinsic motivation, on the other hand, is the propensity to engage in language learning in order to be rewarded, pass an exam or gain a good mark. Those who are extrinsically motivated peg their performance to the levels required to meet a target or secure an award.

A number of researchers (Dörnyei and Ushioda 2011) have investigated the role and effects of motivation and from their work we can gauge its importance. Studies on motivation have indicated that there is a positive correlation between motivation and achievement: highly motivated learners spend attention, effort and energy to complete a task and consequently their achievement is higher than that of their less motivated peers.

MOLT (Motivational Orientation of Language Teaching) is an observation scheme that has been devised (Guilloteaux and Dörnyei 2008) to capture what instructors do to promote motivation among L2 learners. The scheme is based on categories capturing various observable teachers' and learners' behaviour (see Table 3.2) derived from Dörnyei's strategy framework for language classrooms.

Table 3.2 Categories in MOLT

Teacher's motivational teaching practice	Learners' motivated behaviour
Teacher discourse	Attention learners pay in class
Participation structure	Extent of their participation
Encouraging positive respective self-evaluation	Volunteering in tasks
Activity design	

How does integrative and instrumental
motivation play a role in increasing our
success in language learning?

Name three motivational factors that might
have contributed positively to the
acquisition of a second language.

1

2

3

Learning Styles

Language learning styles are considered one of the main factors that
help determine how well L2 learners might acquire a second language
(Cohen 1998). Learning styles can be considered under the following
categories:

- sensory preferences
- personality types
- biological differences

Sensory preferences refer to the ways in which the learner is most
comfortable in processing information and developing skills. Visual learners,
for example, obtain a great deal from visual stimulation, whereas auditory
learners are comfortable without visual input and profit from conversations
and oral stimuli. Kinesthetic and tactile learners enjoy working with tangible
objects such as collages and flashcards.

Personality is another important factor in terms of different learning styles
and consists of four different types (Oxford 1990): extraverted vs introverted;
intuitive-random vs sensing-sequential; thinking vs feeling; and closure-
oriented/judging vs open/perceiving. These different characteristics may or
may not have an impact on the way learners learn languages.

Differences in L2 learning style can also be explained by biological
factors, such as biorhythms, sustenance and location. Biorhythms are cycles
that describe energy levels, and each person's is different. Some learners may
perform better in the morning, others in the evening. Sustenance refers to the

possible need for food or drink that some learners might experience while learning. Location refers to the nature of the learning environment: the temperature, lighting, sounds, and overall the physical environment might have an impact on the language learning experience.

Real-world applications

Input and interaction are key components in SLA. Two main characteristics make input useful for the learner.

First, it must bear meaning, and contain a message that learners can attend to. Features of language make their way to learners' internal learning systems if they have been linked to real-world meaning.

Second, and more importantly, input has to be easily comprehended by learners if acquisition is to happen. Simplifications of the input through the use of contextual props, cues and gestures also promote acquisition. Comprehension activities should be used that initially do not require students to speak in the target language, thus leading to a low filter (high motivation and low anxiety) in the learners. They should be not put under too much pressure to perform at high levels of accuracy and, in the early stages, comprehension is emphasized over production.

Acquisition consists of the building up of form–meaning connections in the learner's head. Features in language (e.g. vocabulary, grammar pronunciation) make their way into the learner's language system only if they are linked to some kind of meaning and are comprehensible to L2 students. As we have discussed, however, not all input – even if it is comprehensible and meaningful – is picked up by learners.

Activity

How do you make input comprehensible and message-oriented in the classroom? Make four suggestions.

1

2

3

4

Instruction has a limited role in SLA. Traditional grammar instruction in particular does little to foster language development and ends up developing a learning-like behaviour. Grammar instruction should be designed so that learners are able to notice and process forms in the input and eventually make correct form–mapping connections. Grammar should also be learned communicatively, with learners being provided with communicative tasks that contain enough samples of the linguistic features they are trying to learn.

What input manipulation techniques do you know?

1

2

3

How do these pedagogical interventions affect the learning of grammar?

Learners must engage in communicative tasks where grammar is enhanced using different input manipulation techniques (e.g. input enhancement, structured input tasks). Given that acquisition can be effectively influenced by manipulating input, grammar tasks should be developed to ensure that learners process input correctly and efficiently. Thus a coherent grammar lesson is one that takes students from processing a grammatical feature in the input to accessing the feature from the internal grammatical system to create output (see Chapter 4).

Activity

Read the following study: VanPatten, B., Collopy, E., Price, J., Borst, S., Qualin, A. (2013). Explicit information, grammatical sensitivity, and the First Noun Principle: a cross-linguistics study in processing instruction. *The Modern Language Journal* 97, 504–525.

- Purpose
- Research questions
- Design
- Results
- Interpretation and significance
- Implications, limitations and further research

Where to find more about this topic

Bardovi-Harlig, K. (2015). One functional approach to SLA. In B. VanPatten and J. Williams (eds.), *Theories in Second Language Acquisition* (2nd ed.; pp.54–74). New York: Routledge.

Benati, A. (2013). *Key Issues in Second Language Teaching*. Sheffield: Equinox.

DeKeyser, R. (2015). Skill Acquisition Theory. In B. VanPatten and J. Williams (eds), *Theories in Second Language Acquisition* (2nd ed.; (pp.94–112). New York: Routledge.

Dörnyei Z., and Skehan P. (2003). Individual differences in second language learning. In C. Doughty and M. Long (eds), *Handbook of Second Language Acquisition*. Oxford: Blackwell.

Dörnyei, Z., and Ushioda, E. (2011). *Teaching and Researching Motivation* (2nd ed.). Harlow: Longman.

Ellis, N., and Wulff, S. (2015). Usage-based approaches to SLA. In B. VanPatten and J. Williams (eds), *Theories in Second Language Acquisition* (2nd ed.; pp.75–93). New York: Routledge.

Gass, S., and Mackey, A. (2015). Input, interaction and output in second language acquisition. In B. VanPatten and J. Williams (eds), *Theories in Second Language Acquisition* (2nd ed.; pp.180–206). New York: Routledge.

Krashen, S. (2009). The comprehension hypothesis extended. In T. Piske and M. Young-Scholten (eds). *Input Matters* (pp. 81–94). Bristol: Multilingual Matters.

Lantolf, J., Thorne, S., and Poehner, E. (2015). Sociocultural theory and second language development. In B. VanPatten and J. Williams (eds), *Theories in Second Language Acquisition* (2nd ed.; pp.207–226). New York: Routledge.

Oxford, R.L. (1990). *Language Learning Strategies: What Every Teacher Should Know*. Boston: Heinle and Heinle.

Pienemann, M., and Lenzing, A. (2015). Processability theory. In B. VanPatten and J. Williams (eds), *Theories in Second Language Acquisition* (2nd ed.; pp.159–179). New York: Routledge.

VanPatten, B. (2003). *From Input to Output: A Teacher's Guide to Second Language Acquisition*. New York: McGraw-Hill.

Van Patten, B. (2015). Input processing in adult SLA. In B. VanPatten and J. Williams (eds), *Theories in Second Language Acquisition* (2nd ed.; pp.113–135). New York: Routledge.

VanPatten, B., and Benati, A. (2015). *Key Terms in Second Language Acquisition* (2nd ed.). London: Continuum.

VanPatten, B., and Rothman, J. (2013). Against rules. In A. Benati, C. Laval, and M. Arche, *The Grammar Dimension in Instructed Second Language Learning* (pp. 15–35). London: Bloomsbury.

VanPatten, B. and Williams, J. (eds) (2015) *Theories in Second Language Acquisition* (2nd ed.). New York: Routledge.

White, L. (2003). *Second Language Acquisition and Universal Grammar*. Cambridge: Cambridge University Press.

White, L. (2015). Linguistic theory, universal grammar, and second language acquisition. In B. VanPatten and J. Williams (eds), *Theories in Second Language Acquisition* (2nd ed.; pp.34–53). New York: Routledge.

How the internal system develops in a second language

4

Introduction

This chapter deals with the most fundamental issue in SLA: the development of the internal language system. Finding out about the rules that L2 learners apply in the process of second language acquisition can happen through collection, analysis and description of samples of learner language. The learner language is called the developing system and/or interlanguage. This chapter illustrates the concept of the developing system, including its characteristics and the processes operating in it, as well as the various types of transfer. In addition, it focuses on explaining how L2 learners consolidate and modify their existing linguistic knowledge and how they generate new knowledge. Further, differences between staged and ordered SLA development are explained. This chapter also deals with cognitive theories of SLA and how they explain the process of language learning. The section on real-world applications summarizes the theoretical explanations (and their practical implications) before presenting their potential applications to the teaching of second languages.

The developing system

The term 'interlanguage' was coined by Larry Selinker (1972) to describe learners' internal developing language system. It refers to a developing language system that shows influences and characteristics of both the L1 system and the new L2 system, which learners are in the process of acquiring.

Other names have been coined to describe and analyze the same language system: 'developing system', 'approximate system' and 'idiosyncratic dialect' have been used to describe the same construct. They all refer to a learner's internal linguistic system, which can be simply described as the mental representation of the language knowledge that learners possess and build from environmental data (input). The system is also responsible for the establishment of sentence-governing relationships (semantic, formal and syntactic) about language structure. After these relationships are established in the learner's internal system, they are subsequently restructured through a number of processes (e.g., hypotheses testing, revising). The concept of hypothesis-testing, for example, explains how the L2 learner progresses along the interlanguage continuum. The developing system is dynamic and continually evolving, moving from lower to higher proficiency levels. Other characteristics of the developing system are systematicity and variability:

- 'systematicity' refers to the processes learners establish in their mental representation and to specific grammatical rules and structures that do not necessarily have to be identical with the rules/structures of the target language. The learners' use of the target language's internal rules may be different to that of a native speaker, but is not haphazard.

- 'dynamicity' refers to the fact that even though learners establish internal systemic rules, these are not static and can be altered with every new exposure, reorganization or formation.

- 'variability' refers to the several factors that may contribute to the development of the interlanguage. These vary from person to person, and may be attributed to the type of the input that the learner has been exposed to as well as to the environment/context in which learners have been put.

According to Selinker (1972), there are five principal processes operating in the learner's developing system:

1 language transfer
2 over-generalization of target language rules
3 transfer of training
4 L2 communication strategies
5 L2 learning strategies

Language transfer

In terms of the influence of the learners' first language on L2 development, the theoretical debate about the role of 'transfer' goes back to the early 1950s when Weinreich (1953: 1) referred to it as 'instances of language deviation from the norms of either language which occur in the speech of bilinguals as a result of their familiarity with more than one language'. Language transfer refers to the effects of one language over the learning of another language. By L1 transfer, we understand the influence of the learner's first language that has been exerted over the acquisition of his/her target language (L2). According to Selinker (1972), language transfer is one of the five central processes to language learning, but it can cause fossilization. This is the mechanism responsible for a permanent cessation of interlanguage learning in spite of the abilities of the learners, the opportunities they have to learn the target language, and their reasons for wanting to learn about and assimilate into the target society (Selinker and Lamendella 1978). Two types of transfer can have an effect on the acquisition of a target language:

1   negative transfer, also known as 'interference'. This is the use of a source-language pattern or rule which leads to an error or inappropriate form in the target language.

2   positive transfer. This type of transfer makes learning easier, and may occur when both the source language and the target language share the same or similar form.

However, not all researchers regard 'transfer' as an influential factor in second language development; see Corder (1967) and Krashen (1981), for example. A broader definition of 'transfer', both positive and negative, is the one offered by Odlin (1989: 27): 'transfer is the influence resulting from similarities and differences between the target language and any other language that has been previously (and perhaps imperfectly) acquired.' Another term referring to transfer and encompassing a broader range of contact effects among the languages under question is 'cross-linguistic influence', as proposed by Sharwood Smith and Kellerman (1986: 1), who argue that 'cross-linguistic influences' are 'those processes that lead to incorporation of elements from one language to another'.

Think of examples for positive and negative transfer effects from your L1 into your L2 that you have experienced through the process of acquiring the L2.

Your L1: _____

Your target language: _____

Positive:

_____
_____
_____

Negative:

_____
_____
_____

Try to explain the possible reasons for these transfer instances.

Possible reasons:

_____
_____
_____

When differentiating between types of cross-linguistic influences in language-acquisition processes in which more than two languages are involved, we can distinguish between two terms: 'reverse' and 'interlanguage' transfer (see Figure 4.1.).

1 'Reverse' transfer refers to instances when the learner transfers from a later acquired language to a previously acquired one, regardless of whether the language is a native or a foreign one. For example, transfer from second language (L2) to first language (L1), third language (L3) to second language (L2) and/or third language (L3) to first language (L1).

2 'Interlanguage' transfer occurs when the learner transfers from one non-native language to another target language. For example, from L2 (first foreign language) to L3 (second foreign language).

Figure 4.1 Cross-linguistic influences according to direction

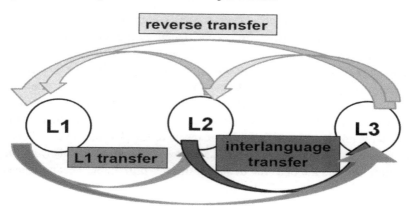

Over-generalization of target language rules

Overgeneralization is a process that takes place during the course of learning a second language where students tend to generalize learned rules for items which are not subject to those rules. Errors of this type are caused by trying to use a rule in a context where it does not belong, and can be found in all linguistic areas, from morphology to syntax, phonology and so on. The following two examples from morphology and syntax illustrate the process:

1 morphology. In English, the forming of plural nouns is normally done by adding -*s*, or -*es* to their corresponding singular forms, so that 'a book' becomes 'books', 'a pen' becomes 'pens' etc. Although there are exceptions – some nouns do not need the -*s* and express the plural with their singular form, as is the case with 'information', while others form in quite a different way, as when 'a mouse' becomes 'mice' or 'a child' becomes 'children' – some learners will tend to overgeneralize the -*s*/-*es* plural rule and apply it to all nouns. So, instead of using 'information' as a plural, they will go ahead and add -*s* to it and thus produce 'informations' or 'childs'.

2 syntax. In a complex sentence containing a relative pronoun as the direct object of the clause, when a human is referred to, you do not always have to use the 'whom' or 'that'. For example, 'The man whom I saw yesterday is 29/The man that I saw yesterday is 29' can also be rendered as 'The man I saw yesterday is 29'. However, the sentence 'The man who met me yesterday is my brother' should not be overgeneralized so as to become 'The man met me yesterday is my brother'.

Transfer of training

The transfer of training occurs when rules communicated by the teacher or a textbook are induced by second language-learners. Such learning outcomes can be positive (i.e. when the induced rule is a correct one) or wrong (i.e. when they lead to errors). For example, if part of a teacher's lesson plan uses key words such as 'past past' for describing the past perfect, the learner can understand that past perfect should be used in all cases for events that occurred a long time ago, but misses the point that the speaker is relating these only to a more recent or foregrounded event. Hence, an isolated statement such as 'We had moved here from Germany in the eighties' may be the outcome of such a transfer of training, i.e. an induced error.

L2 communication strategies

When learners are exposed to a task which requires them to convey meaning but they do not know precisely what words to use, they employ communication strategies. For example, they could point at an object, paraphrase or mime to get their point across. Thus L2 communication strategies are used in all those situations when learners resolve communication problems while their interlanguage system is unequal to the task at hand. Other examples include literal translations, avoidance, language switches (e.g. German 'Hand' instead of English 'hand' with different pronunciations) and approximations (e.g. using 'pipe' instead of 'waterpipe', to name just a few.

L2 learning strategies

Second language-learners consciously use strategies to master the target language. The term 'language learning strategies' has been defined by Oxford, as: 'specific actions, behaviours, steps, or techniques that students use to improve their own progress in developing skills in a second or foreign language' (Oxford 1999: 518).

The way learners select information and filter it from the input also refers to language learning strategies, and it is an important part of understanding the whole SLA process. There have been several suggestions for classifying these according to various criteria (conscious or unconscious, environment- or task-dependent, etc.). Some examples include using mnemonics, flash cards and other devices to remember new words. Language-learners tend to compare L2 language production with the L1 equivalent.

What is a good language-learner, in your opinion?

Research on language learning strategies has a long tradition and it has been subjected to several discussions and criticism. Individuals seem to have personal preferences about how they learn and what strategies they might be willing to employ. The use of learning strategies is also context- and task-dependent. This means that if a certain language learning strategy proves successful for a certain task, it may not be the case for another task or for another learning situation. One of the main critiques of studies on this issues is the source of information that researchers use to derive conclusions about language learning strategies. Normally, researchers use data such as observations, verbal self-reports or think-aloud protocols, all of which have weaknesses in that they provide information and insights into intentional and conscious behaviours only.

The role of output

Output is a key factor in SLA (Gass 1997), and refers to the language which learners produce for a communicative purpose. When producing language (oral and written), L2 learners consolidate and modify their existing linguistic knowledge and they generate new knowledge. This process triggers learners' attention and pushes them to become aware about their needs to convey meanings, or to notice existing gaps in their linguistic knowledge. The Comprehensible Output Hypothesis emerged as a response to Krashen's Input Hypothesis, the original basis of which was that if second-language learners are exposed to a great deal of comprehensible input in a non-stressful situation, they will acquire the new language effectively. This theory did not, however, take into account the role of output and led researchers to question whether comprehensible input really was the vital element in SLA. Swain's Comprehensible Output Hypothesis attempted to investigate and analyze the role of output in language acquisition and was generated from Canadian immersion studies where English native speakers learning French failed to acquire grammatical competence in the target language despite receiving abundant comprehensible input. Swain's principal explanation (Swain 1995) for this was that learners were not being sufficiently pushed to produce language output.

Think of what kind of tasks would be the most suitable ones to get students to produce comprehensible output in the foreign language classroom.

According to the Comprehensible Output Hypothesis, the language that learners produce is seen as an opportunity for them to 'notice' the gap between what they want to say and what they actually can say when interacting with others. Comprehensible output involves the forming and testing of hypotheses, and can have a meta-linguistic function, leading learners to think about language and to use language to talk about language. Thus, language analysis, noticing gaps, making repairs, testing hypotheses about the target language, finding creative solutions, expanding the linguistic existing resources and monitoring are all elements that facilitate SLA.

Output plays a very important role in the learning process, especially as it creates opportunities for learners to receive the feedback they need to verify learning hypotheses. Through production, learners test hypotheses about new language structures and meaning. Further, learners develop automaticity through constant and continuous production in the target language and a shift from meaning-based production to syntactic-focus is meant to be the main outcome.

Stage-like and ordered development

SLA processes are characterized by orders and stages of acquisition (see also Chapter 1). Developmental stages are fixed and cannot be changed (i.e. L2 learners cannot skip one stage and jump to another), regardless of instruction, first language or learning environment (although a degree of variation can occur).

There are two different types of development in SLA: stage-like (specifically sentence structure); and order-like (i.e. A precedes B, B precedes C etc.).

Stage-like SLA development

In the rich body of SLA research, developmental stages (or sequences) have been documented for a number of features (e.g., negation and question formation, as shown in Tables 4.1 and 4.2).

Table 4.1 Stages of negation

Stage	Description	Example
1	'No' is in front of (not attached to) verbs or nouns, sentence initial	*No eat that*
2	'No' moves after the subject of the sentence, and in front of (not attached) to verbs or nouns; 'don't' appears as an alternative to 'no'	*I no eat that*
3	Negation is attached to verbs, modals negated	*I can't eat that*
4	'Do' with attached negation	*I don't eat that* *She didn't eat that*

Table 4.2 Stages of question formation

Stage	Description	Example
1	Single words or sentence fragments	*Four boys?*
2	Declarative word order (no fronting and no inversion)	*The boys throw the shoes?*
3	Fronting (*wh-* fronting but no inversion; *do-* fronting)	*Where the boys are?*
4	Inversion in *wh-* + copula and 'yes/no' questions	*Where are the boys?*
5	Inversion in *wh-* questions (by using 'how')	*How do you get to the boys?*
6	Complex questions (tag questions; negative questions; embedded questions)	*The boys are here, aren't they?*

Although research has indicated that there are systematic and predictable developmental stages in SLA, it does not mean that these stages are like 'locked rooms'. Learners do not jump abruptly from one to another stage, but rather take the 'objects' from one 'room' to the next one, i.e. they produce sentences typical for several different stages. Stages are not characterized by exclusivity but by emergence and increased frequency of a particular structure/form. Sometimes learners may slip back and produce structures from an earlier stage if they are under pressure to produce. For example, if one person produces the majority of the structures typical for stage 3, but occasionally produces a stage 2 structure or a stage 4 structure, it would still mean that the person is in stage 3 overall.

In this context, it is important to mention the 'U-shaped' phenomenon, which refers to a situation in which a learner produces something correctly, reverts to an incorrect version (as a result of having learned something new) but then is eventually able to reproduce the correct form. A classic example given of this can be found in VanPatten and Benati (2010) with regard to the irregular past tense: learners produce highly frequent irregular past tense forms such as 'went' and 'ate' but subsequently begin to produce incorrect irregulars as a result of (unconscious) influence from regular past tense forms (*wented/goed, eated/ated*) before finally re-producing and re-acquiring the correct irregulars. However, we must distinguish here between some correctly produced structures/forms and other *seemingly* 'correctly' produced structures, such as formulaic expressions (parroted /heard from the teacher).

Ordered SLA development

The difference between stage-like and ordered SLA development lies in the focus. The former is concerned with the acquisition of one particular structure over time, while the latter is centred on the relative order in which different structures are acquired over time. Thus, the question of how irregular past tense forms are acquired over time will be pertinent to stage-like development, while the issue of when the irregular past tense is acquired in comparison to other verbal inflections in English (such as third-person singular -*s* and progressive -*ing*) will be pertinent to ordered SLA development. For English verbal inflections, the following acquisition order has been established:

1 progressive -*ing*
2 regular past tense -*ed*
3 irregular past tense
4 third-person singular -*s*

It is important to understand that this stage-like and ordered development do occur simultaneously, i.e. at any given time learner behaviour may exhibit both types. Another difference regarding the focus of interest lies in the fact that ordered SLA development is concerned with morphemes, while staged SLA development is rather concerned with sentence structure. For noun morphemes in English, the following acquisition order has been attested:

plural -*s* → articles → possessive -*s*

Both stage-like and ordered SLA development offer clear evidence that learners must possess internal mechanisms that process and organize language material over time in a systematic manner. What is still an open discussion in the field of SLA are the reasons for such kinds of organization in the learner's mind (e.g. frequency, salience etc.).

MATCHING ACTIVITY: TYPES OF SLA DEVELOPMENT

Write the letter of the correct match for the corresponding type of SLA development in the boxes below:

a) morphemes
b) sentence structure
c) one feature/structure in comparison to other features/structures
d) one feature/structure over time

stage-like SLA development	
ordered SLA development	

L2 learners may exhibit variable performance when entering a specific stage of development or when beginning to acquire a new morpheme or formal feature of language, such as 'Yes see truck' and 'Look my truck'. Researchers distinguish between free and systemic variation. The former is said to be unimportant as it disappears with the reorganization and the development of the L2 system, while the latter refers to the use of two or more formal features that seem to perform the same function, but in reality do not.

Language learning by building 'connections'

Cognitive theories of SLA are based on the assumption that language is acquired not by means of any language-specific device or mechanism, but rather through the employment of general cognitive mechanisms. These are not exclusive to language learning, but rather are common to any kind of learning. They are also responsible for the associations and connections individual learners make through exposure to the language. In other words, learners are exposed to input and they make connections extracted from that input through inducing the appropriate rules. This 'usage-based approach' holds that language learning is a domain-general mechanism and depends on three aspects: social cognition; constraints on working memory; and generalization mechanisms. When discussing usage-based accounts, we must of course mention the theories of constructivism and associative language learning.

The first refers to pairs of form and meaning or function. According to constructivism, everything that can be matched is learnable regardless of complexity. For instance, the adverb 'beautifully' is learned through connecting an adjective with a suffix (-*ly*), but so are complex structures, such as 'Mary gave Jim a kiss' (subject – verb – indirect object – direct object). Constructions are basic symbolic units of language representation. They differ in their degree of complexity and abstraction. In some cases, combinations are possible and in others they are not, depending on the meanings, functions, context and situations. The role of the frequency in which these constructions appear is of specific importance for the constructionist approach. Hence, the more often learners experience and encounter the constructions, the more likely they will be able to access these combinations, i.e. the more those combinations have been entrenched. 'Entrenchment' refers to stabilization of constructions in the memory as a result of repeated exposure to a specific unit. We learn constructions through engaging in conversations. SLA, from a usage-based perspective, can be understood as the emergence of the structural regularities 'from learners' lifetime analysis of the distributional characteristics of the language input' (Ellis 2002: 144).

The more frequently constructions are encountered, the more easily they can be processed. The first time the learner notices a word in the input, a memory is formed whereby the learner binds the features of that word into a specific representation, as can be seen in the phonological sequence \'bȯi\ and the orthographic sequence *boy*. As this representation is built up in the learner's system, so a specific unit is being formed which is used as a detector, and this is activated whenever the features of this sequence are present in the input. The learner's system is tuned to expect constructions that co-occur with one another (form–meaning mappings). The strength of the associations between form and meaning depends on the learner's experiences, i.e. on the frequency of exposure to input. Every aspect of the language is sensitive to frequency, and so we learn language through episodes of processing. The learner's system is tuned to predict the linguistic constructions. According to the usage-based theories of SLA, language structures emerge as a result of interrelated patterns of experience, social interaction and cognitive processes. Every time the language learner/user encounters an exemplar of a construction, the language system activates the memory and compares this exemplar with the previously saved exemplars and retrieves the correct interpretation. The most typical item of the category is called a prototype. For example, people would rather classify sparrows as birds than they would geese as birds. This is done on the basis of conscious distribution of characteristic features, pattern recognition and categorization. This is referred to as Associative Learning Theory, which argues that if the mapping between a cue and its outcome is reliable, the more readily it will be learned. A contingency analysis is needed to understand the reliability between a cue and its outcome, a very simple demonstration can be given through the -s feature at the end of words in English. This particular feature has several potential interpretations: plural of nouns, third-person singular demonstrating the present simple tense of the verb, possession, and so on. If the cue -s is then identified as such, it is obvious that it will/can have many outcomes and that it occurs in many different situations. This contingency analysis demonstrates that this feature will not be easily learned, despite its high frequency.

> **Explain why the connectionist theories behind L2 learning are less plausible than they are for L1 learning.**

The L1 learning experience shapes the L2 learning experience and has an impact on the establishment of associations between the cues and the outcomes, and how learners look for and interpret such cues. Blocking often occurs as a result, whereby redundant cues are overshadowed, and fossilization can creep in, especially in cases where untutored associative L2 learning from naturalistic data takes place.

Another influential usage-based framework is MacWhinney's Competition Model (1987), which offers an explanation for how people come to choose, associate and link appropriate cues when there are multiple cues available. This model originates in first-language acquisition; more precisely, it was developed to account for how monolingual speakers interpret sentences. The main difference between the Competition Model and UG is that the Competition Model does not separate form from function. Hence, the focus is on function and communication rather than sentence structure. The model explains how the strongest cue is selected, and experimental studies based on it have shown that initially learners focus on one thing at a time but in time start to work/focus on more than one cue and are able to build combinations. Let's consider one example from English, which has a rigid word order (SVO):

The cat drinks the milk.

In this case, English native speakers would use various cues to interpret the subject of the sentence. Their first major cue in this sentence is the word order and their knowledge of it – specifically that in an active declarative sentence, the first noun or noun phrase is the subject in the sentence. Second, their lexical knowledge of the meanings of the separate constituents will help determine the cues. The correct interpretation here, of course, is that normally the cat drinks the milk rather than vice versa. Third, English native speakers would also use the animacy factor in determining the cue, i.e. when establishing grammatical relationships, they will ask themselves which of the nouns is animate and whether it could perform an action such as drinking. Finally, the morphology will also be a determining factor; namely the agreement between the cat that is third-person singular and the verb requiring an -*s* in that case. Whether speakers use the same cues from their first language when interpreting sentences in their target language or whether they are employing universal cues is another question. A number of studies have been conducted on this theme and the results generally show that learners employ a meaning-based comprehension strategy rather than a grammar-based one when interpreting sentences in the target language. Correct interpretations of sentences in the target language are accelerated through repeated exposure to input, through establishing regularities, and through reliable input, i.e. (as noted above) the more reliable a cue is, the easier it can be learned. Whether these abilities of associating, choosing or ignoring cues are skills or mental representations will be discussed in the next section.

Language learning as a skill vs mental representation

This section provides a definition of what is meant by 'language as a mental representation' and 'language as a skill'. The first one refers to the abstract, implicit and underlying linguistic system in a speaker's mind/brain (VanPatten and Rothman 2013). It is implicit because we are not aware of it and we cannot describe its content with exact words. A rather different understanding and definition of language is the concept of language as a skill. The origins of this notion are grounded in the cognitive psychology perspective and refer to the speed and accuracy with which individuals perform certain actions. One interesting relation between 'mental representation' and 'skill' is that while skill may involve mental representation, the latter cannot and does not involve skill. For example, in language production it is obvious that at some level a specific mental representation must underlie that language use/production. But not all mental representations are 'transformed' into production or language use. Hence, language learners 'decode' or 'derive' something from the input they are exposed to and then internalize it – a process through which their representation is changed to a certain extent.

In line with the Skill Acquisition Theory (SAT), language learning is seen as similar to the acquisition of any other skill. SAT encompasses the learning of a wide variety of skills, starting from the initial representation of knowledge, through change and development of behaviour to advanced proficiency. In general, however, three stages are being considered common to the learning of skills: declarative; procedural; and automatic or in other words, presentation; practice; and production. These three stages explain the nature of the knowledge being acquired. So, at the beginning of the learning process, students acquire knowledge about something, i.e. declarative knowledge. At this stage, the learner is not even trying to use that 'theoretical' knowledge, but instead acquiring information through observation and through non-active analysis. According to SAT, the next stage (the 'active' stage) is the one in which learners transform their 'theoretical knowledge' or the 'Knowledge about' into behaviour, i.e. they act and use the declarative knowledge and turn it into a procedural knowledge. Neither proceduralization nor automatization happens instantly: once procedural knowledge has been acquired, another series of trials will be needed before that knowledge can be applied with ease and fluency.

Activity

Draw an illustration of where and how the declarative and the procedural knowledge/skill should be placed within the process of automatization.

The danger of deriving implications for teaching or learning based on the Skill Acquisition Theory lies in the issue of overgeneralization being used as an explanation for all SLA processes and related skills. Another danger is linked to the misunderstanding that every kind of complex rule or structure can simply be learned through a theoretical explanation and practice and that the production phase follows gradually. According to the SAT theory, practice gradually decreases reaction time and error rate. Furthermore, SAT claims that declarative/explicit knowledge can be transformed into procedural/ implicit knowledge through the process of automatization, which is a consequence of practice (Richards and Schmidt 2010: 292). The emphasis of the SAT lies in the importance of explicit/declarative knowledge during the initial stages of learning. Hence, when discussing the application of this theory it is important to state its effects for cases where adult L2 learners have a high aptitude, the structures that these adults learn are simple and these adults are at early stages of learning within an instructional context/setting.

Can you think of reasonable criticism for the Skill Acquisition Theory?

Even the most basic problems of this theory for the field of SLA in general are concerned with definitions of the terms 'skill', 'practice' and 'automatization'. The SAT theory seems to support the strong interface position, which claims that explicit knowledge can be transformed into implicit knowledge.

Moreover, the process of learning is impacted by affective factors, i.e. practice is not the most important element and it does not always necessarily make perfect. This holds true in situations where the learner is exhausted or under pressure. Krashen's idea of the low affective filter is useful here: this theory disregards the idea that the process of learning is different depending on the task at hand. In other words, it ignores the possibility of achieving the same outcome but through different 'means' than 'standard' practice in the SAT sense, for example by being creative. Another problem with this theory is its validity and objectivity. In order to be able to prove its arguments, a number of methodological conditions must be met, yet it is very difficult for researchers to assemble enough long-term study participants for their individual variables to be adequately explained or accounted for.

The most important criticism of the Skill Acquisition Theory has been suggested by Ellis and Shintani (2013), who claim that the SAT fails to explain the sequence of acquisition. Furthermore, they do not agree that learning starts with declarative knowledge. As evidence they offer the fact that not all aspects of grammar learning necessarily involve explicit knowledge alone, stating instead that much grammar is learned incidentally, as is vocabulary. Such types of learning do not require a declarative stage. The usage-based accounts of language acquisition claim that incidental associative learning provides the groundwork for language acquisition, and that the analysis and use of input allows us to become fluent in our L1s. In other words, SAT supporters do not regard language as unique and uniquely acquired; for them, it is a skill like any other. Obviously, this claim does not adequately explain the L2 process and thus the theoretical applications of the SAT to SLA face several obstacles. The SAT fails to explain the developmental sequences of SLA as well as why some forms are easily and more quickly acquired than others. Most importantly, it does not explain why L1 transfer differs for SLA and why it varies from case to case and from situation to situation.

Real-world applications

When attempting to find real-world applications based on theoretical concepts, such as the learner's developing system, the role of output, types of language development, types of learning and the nature of learning, we need answers to several important questions:

- Why do teachers need to know about the developing system of learners and how does this knowledge help them with their teaching procedures?
- What options can teachers draw on to have students produce comprehensible output?
- How can teachers benefit from the usage-based accounts of SLA?
- Does the Skill Acquisition Theory offer any new implications for language teachers?
- How can classroom opportunities be enriched and created?

For each of these questions we suggest real-world applications based on the theoretical concepts linked to these issues and discussed in this chapter.

Why do teachers need to know about the developing system of learners and how does this knowledge help them with their teaching procedures?

The study of the developing system of learners helps teachers to evaluate their teaching procedures and gauge how they compare to their expectations of, and what is possible in, a classroom situation. Teachers need to understand that the rules and structures presented in textbooks do not resemble the organization of the linguistic knowledge in their learners' minds. Learners need to be exposed to sufficient input, which is needed to develop mental representations about language. This clearly has an impact on the type of activities teachers will develop and decide to use in their lessons. But what kinds of activities promote development of mental representation and which promote development of communicative ability (bearing in mind that mental representation and communicative ability differ)? This question has been answered by VanPatten (2014: 25):

> Clearly, input-oriented activities help to develop mental representation. Interactive activities help to develop communicative ability. In either case, we must keep in mind our definition of communication: the expression and interpretation of meaning in a given context. Thus, whether activities are input oriented, interactive, or some combination, the expression and interpretation of meaning within the classroom should be the core of these activities.
>
> *VanPatten 2014: 25*

Understanding how learners allocate their attention during online processing of input will enable teachers to become more aware of students' needs and sensitive when planning their teaching. This will require a good deal of change and sacrifice, but will be worth it if the outcomes are positive.

Knowing about the developing system helps teachers discover, through learners' errors, about their ability to use the target language and their knowledge of it. Such knowledge helps teachers to differentiate between the various types of errors displayed, and whether at that particular stage of L2 development such errors are naturally to be expected. Ideally, teachers will realize that an increased error rate is necessarily indicative of a lack of practice or as part of a transfer from the L1, but rather that it might be a sign of progress (active mental process of hypothesis-testing, resulting in overgeneralization). The learners are actually working with the target language but perhaps trying to use a rule in a context where it does not belong.

As is clear from SLA research, learners pass through certain developmental stages regardless of their first language of level of instruction received and it is important that teachers bear this in mind, accepting the fact that the development is natural and that particular 'errors' are expected. Consequently, trying to correct a developmental error cannot be beneficial at that stage, as research findings show that L2 learners from different L1 backgrounds often display the same kinds of errors. Being aware of an L2 learner's developing system will help teachers to understand that he or she might just be attempting to discover how the target language actually operates.

What options can teachers draw on to have students produce comprehensible output?

The idea of 'comprehensible output' refers to creating opportunities for learners to 'notice' the gap between what they want to say and what they actually can say when interacting with others; in other words, they are 'pushed' to think about language and to use it to talk about language. In so doing they become aware that creative solutions are needed and that they must acquire the means to expand their existing linguistic repertoire.

> Based on your own experience as a second language learner, think of the best task/activity you were introduced to and explain why this has helped you to produce comprehensible output.

Although several techniques can contribute to comprehensible output production, we offer here a brief overview of the benefits of 'collaborative tasks', 'intelligent guessing' and 'dictogloss' procedures.

Collaborative tasks (Kowal and Swain 1997) (such as 'information gap' activities) are one of the best ways to help students produce comprehensible output. Even in situations where learners are completely inexperienced with a particular language feature/form, they can work with a partner and benefit from that person's knowledge, becoming more proficient in the process. While such pair-work is ostensibly more beneficial for the weaker student or novice learner, it can also help strong students by consolidating their knowledge. Ideally this work will be motivating for both partners.

Intelligent guessing (Angelovska and Hahn 2014) is a process of challenging and understanding how the target language functions by discovering gaps in one's own output through interlanguage monitoring. The language teacher and the learner engage in an inductive guessing language play with clearly defined three-fold roles: the teacher acts as detector (of, for example, grammatical problems or negatively transferred features), setter of challenges and hint-giver, while the learner acts as thinker, decision-maker and responder. The goal is to raise language awareness by exploiting all the means available.

A similar type of negotiation, feedback with negotiation, was explained and tested by Nassaji (2011), who suggests (2011: 323) the following procedure. The teacher addresses the target language error through negotiation by encouraging and pushing the learner further to discover and correct the error, using step-by-step guided help and scaffolding. The teacher begins with indirect and implicit feedback and moves progressively towards more direct and more explicit help as required until the error is resolved. The difference to the previous technique is that in the former the teacher has the role of helping the learner to resolve the error on his/her own without giving any explicit help. The focus in the intelligent guessing is put on giving indirect help.

Dictogloss (Swain 1998) is a procedure in which the learner is encouraged to focus on output through reflecting on it. The teacher reads a certain text twice; students listen to the first reading without doing anything but during the second jot down some key words which will help them to reconstruct the text. Once they have attempted this, their versions are analyzed and compared with the original, and they get the opportunity to focus on the language and refine it. Finally, we conclude with VanPatten's advice:

> When learners speak, they speak to engage in communication; they don't speak to practice something. Currently, too much of language pedagogy has learners engaged in output to practice something; this 'communication' is subservient to learning vocabulary and grammar. The role of output and interaction in communication and language acquisition suggests that this is backwards.
>
> *VanPatten 2014: 26*

How can teachers benefit from the usage-based accounts of SLA?

There are several conclusions to be drawn from a discussion of implications for teaching from the usage-based perspectives on SLA. First, teachers need to create situations in which interaction plays a central role and in which they can bring to learners' attention additional sources to help them notice cues. Second, the teacher must ensure that the input is presented very frequently. Third, the teacher should make use of categorization options and structure the presented input accordingly, so that learners can use the appropriate 'domain-general' mechanisms to learn. For example, language could be presented to the students as 'chunks'. These input delivery methods do not present learners with explicit information, however, nor do they offer to the learner explicit feedback supported by metalinguistic comments.

If we are to understand the implications of the usage-based theory for teaching foreign languages, we have to follow the idea of inductive discovery-based learning in which learners come to discover gaps on their own by being given meaningful material to work with. The question of what the usage-based theory offers for teachers in terms of manner of presenting language to the learners leads to an important implication from the competition model, according to which teachers must present one thing at a time at the initial stages of language learning and then gradually increase items in combinations.

Does the Skill Acquisition Theory offer any new implications for language teachers?

Discussing the possibilities of integrating insights from the Skill Acquisition Theory into the classroom will inevitably have implications for three main aspects: practice; declarative knowledge; and procedural knowledge. According to the SAT, practice is crucial. Behaviours acquired through repeated practice bring about the restructuring of the declarative knowledge, which in turn becomes a proceduralized skill and requires less working memory capacity. Hence the SAT claims that explicit teaching is beneficial and that students should be given enough time to develop their skills. According to the SAT, if errors occur, learners need to be corrected. The types of activities being suggested here range from 'communicative drills', in which learners repeat words and expressions without focusing explicitly on form, to 'spot the difference' and 'memory games'. During these, learners should not pay attention to the form being practised, i.e. they need to de-focus from the form and prioritize the task at hand. However, what is not clear about the SAT is how teachers should help learners to transfer from declarative knowledge to procedural skill within various contexts, in particular from the classroom to the real world.

REFLECTION

What is your view of 'error correction' and 'de-focusing'? Do you support the SAT's arguments? Why/why not?

To sum up, teachers need to be equipped with knowledge about how their learners' interlanguage system develops over time in order to be able to understand their output, the type of errors they are displaying, the difficulties they are faced with and their progression over time.

How can classroom opportunities be enriched and created?

Teachers need to understand that input and output are the foundations of a successful second language acquisition process. Moreover, they need to make sure that they provide appropriate and meaningful input that has been tailored to the needs of their learners, because acquisition is input-dependent. Input matters for both instructed and natural contexts as it is the primary material learners need to build up their developing systems. One technique employed to structure input in a helpful way is the 'input enhancement' pedagogical intervention, which concerns formal features of language and is a kind of focus on form. It is necessary to understand a relevant shift in focus for teachers that has developed in recent years and for that purpose we quote VanPatten and Benati here:

> Such questions drove researchers to examine the effects not of instruction more generally but of particular kinds of instructional interventions; those that were both input oriented and meaning based. These interventions include such things as text enhancement, processing instruction, input flood, recasts, and others (see input enhancement as well as focus on form). It is not clear whether these more acquisition-driven approaches to instructional intervention actually affect SLA in any significant way, but it is clear that the field has shifted from the more global 'Does instruction make a difference?' to more specific 'Does manipulating input make a difference?'
>
> *VanPatten and Benati 2010: 52*

In other words, teachers should contribute to the process of creating an implicit system in their learners' minds and understand that acquisition is not explicit learning. They should also distance themselves from the idea that the explicit knowledge they are trying to install in their learners' heads will ever become implicit knowledge. This should not be taken as meaning that explicit knowledge is not helpful, but rather that teachers should understand that languages are not learnt by practising rules alone, and that output is needed for learners to develop appropriate skills linked to the process of making meaning. In addition, teachers should know that the process of acquisition has been constrained in many ways and they need to understand the 'equipment' that their learners bring to the task of learning a particular language. This implies that teachers need to understand the process of SLA in its fullest before they approach the task of teaching a foreign language or even preparing the content, materials, tasks and activities for the foreign-language learning classroom. Based on such insights into the psycholinguistic basis of the SLA process, teachers will be able to accommodate the content of their teaching, to adjust teaching procedures, materials and approaches, to give appropriate feedback and to offer the support necessary for their students to become successful language learners.

Where to find more about this topic

Ellis, N. C. (2012). Frequency-based accounts of SLA. In S. M. Gass and A. Mackey (eds), *Handbook of Second Language Acquisition* (pp. 193–210). London: Routledge.

Ellis, R., and Shintani, N. (2013). *Exploring Language Pedagogy Through Second Language Acquisition Research*. London: Routledge.

Eskildsen, S. W. (2009). Constructing another language: usage-based linguistics in second language acquisition. *Applied Linguistics*, 30, 335–357.

VanPatten, B. (2010). The two faces of SLA: Mental representation and skill. *International Journal of English Language Studies*, 10, 1–18.

How learners learn to communicate in a second language

5

Introduction

Understanding the knowledge possessed by a competent second language learner and his/her ability to use that knowledge in a communicative situation – and most importantly, how that knowledge is acquired – will be the central part of this chapter. It offers an explanation of how individuals learn to communicate appropriately in a second language, how they socialize and adapt to the rules of the particular speech community and what comprises the construct of communicative competence. This chapter entails accounts of functionalist approaches to language. The concept-oriented approach is explained and the roles of interaction and socialization in the process of a second language acquiring (form–function mappings and expression of meanings) are examined from functionalist perspectives. The SLA process is also influenced by cultural practices, explained through Vygotsky's Socio-Cultural Theory, Giles' Accommodation Theory and Schumann's Acculturation Model. The importance of extending SLA in today's multilingual world will be explained through a short introduction into the field of multilingualism, where we will attempt to distinguish between terms such as bilingualism, heritage language and multilingualism. A special focus is given to terms such as 'multilingual competence' and the Dynamic System Theory, and official numbers regarding multilingualism in the European Union will be presented. Finally, the last section of this chapter covers the real-world applications of all theories and approaches, and practical implications for teaching will be illustrated.

The construct and components of communicative competence

Sociolinguistics is a study that investigates how language functions in society. It also covers the interaction between linguistic and social variables, as well as how language is realized in social and cultural contexts and how that changes among groups and communities over time. In order to be accepted in a community, one needs to possess certain skills and competences. Thus, when it comes to discussing the purpose of learning a foreign language, highlighting the role of communicative competence is immensely important.

Communicating in a foreign language entails a successful mastery of a variety of 'tools', skills and sub-competences, learning how to choose the right language means, style, genre and tone. Thus, just as Chomsky's notion of 'linguistic competence' regulates communication, so using that competence *appropriately* contributes to successful communication. To that end, it is vital to highlight the difference between the terms 'competence' and 'performance'. The former denotes an individual's knowledge of how a language functions and its rules, as well as which form or structure is appropriate in which context or situation. The latter is actually the demonstration of that competence. In other words, performance is the practical use of one's knowledge.

The concept of communicative competence was introduced by Dell Hymes 1966, just a year after Noam Chomsky had introduced his idea of linguistic competence. Hymes' original idea was that being able to communicate effectively in a foreign language requires more than grammatical competence, and that learners also need to have a wider knowledge base in order to be able to adjust their language to the speech community in which they happen to be. In other words, students need to know the rules of their target language's speech community, how language is used by the members of that community and how they as learners can accomplish their communication goals. Despite numerous misinterpretations of this approach, communicative competence does not diminish the importance of grammatical knowledge, and it remains an important part of Hymes' theory. Communicative competence appeared in, and was re-conceptualized in, the work of Canale and Swain (1980), Swain (1985), Bachman (1990), Bachman and Palmer (1996), Celce-Murcia, Dörnyei, and Thurrell (1995) among many. Canale and Swain's model has been modified over the years, but continues to dominate the field of second and foreign language acquisition.

The four components of the concept (see Figure 5.1) according to Canale (1983) are linguistic, sociolinguistic, discourse and strategic competence.

Grammatical competence refers to learners' knowledge of grammar and vocabulary as well as the conventions associated with written language,

Figure 5.1 Communicative competence (adapted from Canale and Swain 1980)

such as orthography. Grammatical competence also entails phonological knowledge, such as tone, pitch and rhythm, phonetic knowledge, i.e. knowledge of sounds and their pronunciation, morphological knowledge (the rules that govern the formation of words through inflection or derivation), syntactic knowledge (the rules that help us to combine words and phrases and form sentences) and semantic knowledge (the knowledge of what meaning to convey and therefore the best words to choose).

Sociocultural competence refers to knowledge of sociolinguistic rules of language use, or being able to use language appropriately, to initiate a conversation in a correct way and to respond to specific language, taking into account factors such as genre and register. Correct usage depends on the context, the topic, and the 'power' relationship between the interlocutors. Participants in a conversation have expectations about what rights they have in the exchange, and they manifest these differential power relations through language forms. In this sense, language becomes the most powerful weapon of social behaviour. In addition to these factors, knowing about the culture of the speech community means being aware of appropriateness too, and this includes knowledge about what is polite or impolite, politically correct, friendly, ironic etc. and how to express that knowledge through language.

Discourse competence refers to knowing how to work with written and oral modes of communication both in production and comprehension. In short, that means being able to combine the structures of a particular language coherently and cohesively, i.e. knowing how to organize words, phrases and sentences in order to produce different types (genres) of texts, such as speeches, poems, emails, newspaper articles, journal articles etc.

Strategic competence refers to the ability to recognize situations in which miscommunication or communication breakdowns have occurred, and being able to sort out the ensuing unfortunate situations. This involves being able to 'paraphrase' when a word is missing, asking for clarifications, explaining what was meant, using slower speech, using gestures, taking turns in conversation so that the communication channels are kept open, and restoring communication.

Both the model itself and the various modifications thereof have been criticized for not having included the pragmatic component. Although the sociolinguistic component is said to entail pragmatic competence, the latter was not explicitly considered to be a component of communicative competence until the late 1980s. In addition, no indication was given of how to link communicative competence and its components to the four skills in language teaching (speaking, writing, reading and listening) in any of the models.

Widdowson (1983) was the first to point out the terminological differences between 'knowing' and 'applying'. He stresses the importance of actual language use (performance) in comparison to competence (knowledge). In other words, he distinguishes between 'competence' and 'capacity'. The former refers to learners' knowledge of linguistic and sociolinguistic conventions and the latter to ability or procedural knowledge. According to Widdowson (1983), 'ability' differs from 'competence'. Widdowson's insights motivated fruitful discussions about the role of teachers in fostering the teaching and learning of communicative competence within the foreign language classroom, mainly in the context of the communicative language teaching approach with a clear focus on interaction.

'Interaction' refers to the conversational processes that learners take part in. In these processes, learners learn about concepts such as the appropriateness and correctness of utterances (or the lack thereof) by means of interactional feedback that provides them with information on how successful their productions have been. It is essential that learners take part in these interactions if they are to understand how to negotiate (or figure out) meaning. The negotiation of meaning is the process in which learners attempt to compensate for linguistic (and even) sociolinguistic inadequacies through interactional modifications and the use of various communication strategies that overcome a breakdown in communication. The use of these effective strategies in the negotiation of meaning is seen as an element of strategic competence (Canale 1983). On the other hand, if learners are exposed to negative evidence, that may guide them to notice errors or failures in the flow of communication. It is not a question that interactional input is more facilitative than simplified input. However, Doughty and Long (2003) provide some insights into the existing problematic discussions about the input and interaction within interactional perspectives. Their argument refers to the difficulty of linking the effects of learning to dialogue exchanges alone. In other words, it is difficult to say whether a feature was learned as a result of negotiation of meaning or whether it is a mere imitation or repetitive act.

What *is* for sure is that interaction has a facilitative role in the comprehension process.

SLA happens through conversation

Functionalist approaches to language consider that its primary focus is communication. The functionalist models of language analysis date back to the early twentieth century; more precisely, they are rooted within the scope of the Prague School of Linguistics. Researchers within SLA functionalist approaches are concerned with the methods that learners use to convey meanings and to achieve their communication goals.

It is important to note here that the functionalism and the generativism are ideologically different. Functionalists characterize the functionalist view to be an addition to the UG approach and for them, the knowledge of language is demonstrated only by actual language use. Specifically, the difference between the two approaches lies in the way each views language: for functionalists, language is a system of communication while for generativists it is a set of rules (with distinct innate language competence for humans). Functionalists focus on the conveyed meanings in the different contexts and see forms of natural languages as created, governed, constrained, acquired and used with the one aim of communication.

Functionalism recognizes no sharp distinction between performance (what the learner shows and displays in actual language use) and competence (what the learner actually knows, the knowledge s/he possesses) in comparison to the generativists.

The focus of researchers operating within the functionalism framework is the development of interlanguage over time, particularly in terms of form–function and function–form mappings. These mappings can best be illustrated through a procedure in which a certain grammatical form is focused on in order to discover how it functions. For example, the English past simple tense for regular verbs, i.e. the first observed function in the acquisition of -*ed*, denotes a completion of past events and the second function is to indicate a main event in the story.

When looking at the acquisition of tense and aspect, the Aspect and Discourse Hypotheses both merit a mention. The Aspect Hypothesis claims that both first and second language learners are influenced by the inherent semantic characteristics of verbs during the initial stage of acquiring tense and aspect markers (Andersen and Shirai 1994). This view is semantically bound and thus focuses on the influences of lexical aspects of the verbs on the acquisition of tense–aspect morphology. Studies on tense–aspect marking within the L2 development of two English native speakers of English who are acquiring Spanish, shows that the past-tense markers emerged with punctual verbs (which denote an action in a moment, for example, *break*) and achievement verbs (which indicate the beginning and end of an action, for example, *start, finish* etc.) and that the markers for imperfect emerged with verbs that indicate state (and which denote persistence over time without change, e.g. *seem, know, need* etc.). Andersen (1984) has postulated an order of developmental stages in which the development of the past tense follows this order:

achievement verbs → accomplishment verbs → state verbs

In general, findings emerging from this line of research demonstrate the following:

- past/perfective morphology can be found in punctual and accomplishment verbs;
- imperfective morphology can be found with durative and stative verbs;
- progressive morphology can be found with durative verbs (denoting activity).

To investigate the functions of a certain language we need to have samples of that language in context, in the form of discourse. The Discourse Hypothesis differs from the Aspect Hypothesis in that it does not focus on the lexical meaning of verbs, but rather on the structure of discourse in terms of the background (supporting information) and foreground (new information) of the events within it. According to the Discourse Hypothesis, 'learners use emerging verbal morphology to distinguish foreground from background in narratives' (Bardovi-Harlig 1994: 43). Later studies by Bardovi-Harlig (1998: 498) support both hypotheses (the Aspect and the Discourse). More precisely in terms of simple past marking, she found that achievement verbs are inflected for the simple past, regardless of the type of information provided in the discourse (fore- or background). These are then followed by accomplishment verbs. Verbs denoting activities are the least likely to carry simple past.

A well-formed discourse entails new and old information, but the flow of that information is presented in a coherent way. For example, the difference between the following two fully grammatical sentences ('Mary bought an iPhone' and 'She bought it') is that only the first has clear information and the second can be understood only if the context and the previous information is known. Pragmatics, a linguistic area, deals with investigation of language in context and with the ways in which pragmatic knowledge is demonstrated in actual use. The use of pragmatic knowledge in language over time has been a central focus of L2 research from a functionalist perspective, and Givón (1979) is a particular proponent of a distinction between pragmatic and syntactic modes. According to this view, speakers move from a pragmatic (or pre-syntactic) mode of communication, in which they rely mainly on context clues rather than on structure and syntax, to a syntactic mode, in which they are able to construct sentences in a more grammatically correct way. Reasons for this shift range from speakers' need to sound like interlocutors, the economization of language use, or even communicative failure. The question of *how* individuals move from the pragmatic to the syntactic mode has not really been fully explained to date within functionalist approaches, but this does not imply that the breadth of functionalism in L2 research is limited. On the contrary, different approaches within the functionalism framework investigate different functions. One of the earliest, the Prague school of Linguistics, explored sentence perspectives, topic, text types etc. Even studies on processing have been conducted within the functionalism framework. In this respect, it is also worth mentioning MacWhinney's Competition Model (see Chapter 4).

A specific functionalist approach of the function–form type is the concept-oriented approach. This argues that a function, concept or meaning is identified by the speaker and its expressions investigated, which leads to a focus on form–function mapping. In this way, a concept can be time or temporality or subsets, like past or futurity. For example, the concept of 'time' can be linguistically expressed/encoded through linguistic devices such as tense, grammatical aspect, lexical aspect, temporal adverbials, temporal particles and discourse principles. Hence, the concept-oriented approach is interested in the devices and means users employ to express meanings and uses a multilevel analysis to explore this. The basic tenet of the concept-oriented approach is that second language learners already have access to previous linguistic and cognitive experience and the only task they have is to express meanings in their second language. The idea is that language serves communication and form serves function. A very important aspect of the concept-oriented approach, and one that has crucial implications for language teaching professionals, is the learners' need to express a certain concept. This means that teachers must create situations and materials that push learners to express meaning.

Analysis of the concept-oriented approach seeks to explain the ways in which meanings are expressed at a given point and how the expression of a certain concept changes over time. It is important to highlight that the concept-oriented approach does not investigate forms, but rather concepts. The usage of the various linguistic devices depends on their 'functional load', in other words, meanings for which there are reasonable (grammatical and communicative) means of expressions are less likely than others to promote the acquisition of new form. For example, the present perfect (*has done*) and the past perfect (*had done*) both express the same complexity in terms of form, but a study by Bardovi-Harlig (2000) has shown that even when both are taught in the same time, the present perfect emerges earlier in the acquisition process. The explanation for this is given in the functional load, in that the present perfect does not have any functional equivalent able to express the same meaning. The meaning of the past perfect, on the other hand, can be expressed through a verb in the past simple with an additional adverbial. If we take another example referring to the past, in a sentence which expresses a finished action in the past, use of 'yesterday' as a temporal adverbial will indicate a high functionality. According to the concept-oriented approach, second language learners move through certain stages when expressing meanings:

pragmatic → lexical → morphological

The pragmatic stage is characteristic of the use of chronological order or discourse that provides the temporal reference. During the lexical stage, learners use temporal adverbials to establish a time orientation, while during the morphological stage they use verb inflections to indicate time relations.

Functionalist studies analyze language data in a wide range of natural situations, from narrations to the retellings of stories or short film extracts, asking students to make predictions and other communicative activities in which a need to express meaning has been created. It is important to note that when the analysis of results is reported in functionalist studies, no details are given about whether learners score correctly or not. What functionalists are interested in is how learners construct their language. For some researchers, especially those who are new to this approach, it is often difficult to ignore form and to focus solely on interpreting performance in terms of meaning rather than accuracy. The longitudinal design, favoured by the concept-oriented approach, allows the investigation of a range of learners' variables.

Think of the three most important learner variables in line with the concept-oriented approach:	Discuss whether these can be observed longitudinally and if yes, how.
Variable 1:	
Variable 2:	
Variable 3:	

Studies within the concept-oriented approach usually take as evidence longitudinal production data, i.e. language used in communication over time. This approach encourages the investigation of sequences in the interlanguage developing system, from the earliest stage to the advanced stage. The researcher most commonly associated with the concept-oriented approach is Bardovi-Harlig. One theme being investigated within this approach is main focus, and specifically how learners express it, how its means of expression interact and how that expression changes over time. Based on these mappings, Andersen (1984, 1990) has formulated two principles: the one-to-one principle and multifunctionality principle. The one-to-one principle refers to the construction of an interlanguage in such a way that one intended meaning is expressed with just one clear form or construction. The multifunctionality principle usually applies at later stages of L2 acquisition when learners begin to broaden their repertoire of functions and forms, and get to know expressions of meanings in various contexts and through diverse forms. The multifunctionality principle refers to one form being mapped onto many meanings and one meaning being expressed through many forms. An appropriate example could be the use of present progressive -*ing* for ongoing events only, although the same form is used to express futurity. This is, of course, not known by learners during the initial stages of L2 acquisition, when they associate only the form 'will' with the future. Later, as they pass through more advanced stages, they work with more developed and complex mappings by employing various linguistic devices. Another example of a functionalist analysis is the expression of plurality. In the early stages, learners may map three forms onto the concept of 'plurality': quantifiers; numerals; and plural morphology. In this sense, noun phrases such as *four girl, many boy* and *three girls* will be correct in the sense that 'successful expression of plurality' has taken place as the number denotes plurality. According to functionalists, learners will happen to balance this use within time and the marker –*s* for plurality will become dominant, i.e. next to the number they will be able to attach –*s* to the noun. According to the concept-oriented approach, successful communication is what motivates learners to reach the more advanced stage. Hence, each next stage would imply that learners use a more varied range of expressions for meaning and are less dependent on help from their partners in communication, i.e. they are communicating more independently. This insight is in line with Selinker's interlanguage concept and the changing learner varieties, whereby functionalists emphasize the specificity of the learner language as a system in its own right and discourage any possible form of comparison between such a system and the target-language norm against which development will be measured.

It is essential that the effects of instruction are discussed within the concept-oriented approach. Related studies support the view that instruction has a limited impact; in other words, research claims that in cases where instructed and uninstructed learners were compared in their early acquisition periods, they were at the same level (Bardovi-Harlig 2000). This is very much in line with Pienemann's Teachability Hypothesis (Pienemann 1998; Pienemann and Lenzing 2015), which argues that not everything that is taught can necessarily be learned. In other words, the effects of instructed language-learning on the development of the interlanguage system depends on the developmental stage of the learner. Hence, if the learner is not ready, he or she will not benefit from instruction. But even if learners happen to be developmentally ready for the instruction, it can still only go so far (in that learners may not immediately be able to map form and meaning) and naturally success levels will vary among learners.

The work of Klein and Dimroth (2009) is important here as it gives clear insights into the characterization of instruction. According to them, instruction is disadvantageous to untutored learners' acquisition process with regard to communication. Klein and Dimroth outline three disadvantages of instructed learning in comparison to untutored acquisition. Classroom teaching usually offers pre-processed language, i.e. language that is not communicated in spontaneous ways as it might be in real-life situations. For example, in the classroom, correct provision comes externally (through the teacher) but outside ('natural') learners develop their own forms of assessment by asking themselves whether they are understood, whether they understand and whether their way of speaking is exactly as that of their interlocutors. These aspects refer to the centrality of communication within the concept-oriented approach.

In the table below, suggest some weaknesses and strengths of functionalism.

Weaknesses	Strengths

SLA occurs through socialization

If communication is at the heart of the functionalist approach to SLA, the socio-cultural approaches see 'socialization through culture' as a central focus in their explanations for language development. The Socio-Cultural Theory (SCT) has its origins in the work of the Russian psychologist Vygotsky (1978) and argues that humans' mental functioning is a process that is organized by cultural activities and concepts, i.e. individuals use existing knowledge in order to create new, cultural insights that help them to monitor and control their behaviour. The developmental process of speaking happens through our participation in cultural and linguistic settings. According to the SCT, human neurobiology is a necessary condition for higher mental processes, but our human cognitive activity develops only through interactions in specific settings (family, school etc.). Individual development is seen in material, social and historical contexts. The roots of the SCT are based on principles advanced in Marxism: the idea that human consciousness is mainly a social and human activity is mediated by language and the environment.

The central construct of the theory is mediation. According to the SCT, the human mind comprises lower-level mental processes, but the capacity of human consciousness to control biology through using higher-level symbols (such as language, logic, categorization etc.) is distinctive. These symbols are developed within historical, cultural and developmental contexts, which link the individual to the wider social world. Three types of regulation are distinguished within the scope of the SCT: object-, other- and self-regulation. Object-regulation refers to activities in which objects in the environment are required to regulate a certain language or cognitive activity, for example, looking up a word in an online dictionary. Other-regulation refers to how people accelerate a certain language or cognitive process, for example, receiving feedback on a speech they've given or a word they've pronounced incorrectly.

HANDS-ON

Think of one activity for strengthening the communication skills of second-language learners based on the SCT. Write down the instructions for the teacher and the learners and describe the activity.

Instructions for the teacher:

Instructions for the learners:

Description of the activity:

The Zone of Proximal Development (ZPD; see Figure 5.2) fits well with the other-regulation stage if linked to second language learning, because the support offered by the expert is central to an individual's development. In the case of self-regulation, the individual has internalized specific forms of mediation which help him or her in a certain activity. In the process of conducting that activity, the individual learns how to control resources and activities more effectively and how to become more proficient in the use of the mediated resources. It is important to understand that the process of self-regulation is not static, though. Depending on various situations, one can revert back to other- or object-regulation when confronted with difficult communicative scenarios. Task demands can also influence the transition from one regulation type to another, and in accordance with these the individual can move through the three different regulation types.

Figure 5.2 Zone of proximal development (ZPD) and tasks

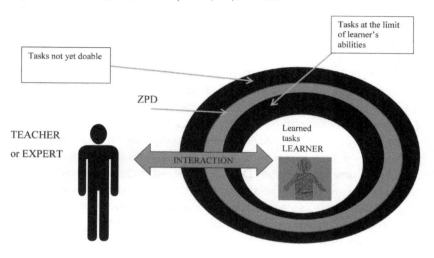

According to Vygotsky, human consciousness entails processes of planning (composed of memorized previous actions), attention to relevant aspects of communication, but ignores irrelevant, rational thinking, logical observing and predicting. The inner, self-directed use of language as a symbolic tool for cognitive regulation is referred to as 'inner speech'. The process of learning how to communicate appropriately also entails private or inner speech in which self-regulated language has been externalized. The socio-cultural theory proposes that second languages can be acquired through social interactions, and thus language teachers must offer students a range of activities that facilitate these.

The ZPD represents the relation and the distance between the point at which an individual is able to function independently by using his or her independent problem-solving skills and the point at which an individual has been supported by an expertise of another peer (or peers) and/or a more advanced expert/teacher. ZPD has proved attractive for educators and psychologists because of the aspect of 'assisted performance' that is an integral part of its construct and which unites the two important elements of developmental potential and achieved development. The finding that distinguishes Vygotsky from Piaget is the importance of school instruction and the benefits it has for individual development. It is clear that the potential of the ZPD, and the role of corrective feedback in tutor–learner interactions, have proved to be influential aspects in SLA. Findings have shown that certain mechanisms prove helpful with regard to the benefits of the ZPD, but they must be scaled appropriately, i.e. starting with implicit feedback before moving to explicit correction. Concrete suggestions of how frequently, and to what extent, teachers should give feedback must be considered in language teaching.

Learners' development within the ZPD does not rely on observations made about the performance of the individuals *per se*. Another important element that offers us an insight into how far an individual has developed is the locus of control for that performance, i.e. who (other-regulation) or what (object-regulation) do learners need to progress (peers or an expert, perhaps), or if they can help themselves (self-regulation). It is important to acknowledge that although the terms of 'scaffolding' and Krashen's '*i+1*' are associated with the ZPD, they differ from it. 'Scaffolding' refers to any kind of adult–child or expert–novice assisted performance. The focus does not lie in any mediation, quality or even type of assistance but rather in the *amount* of assistance one requires in order to progress. Donato (1994: 40) defines scaffolding as a 'situation where a knowledgeable participant can create supportive conditions in which the novice can participate, and extend his or her current skills and knowledge to higher levels of competence'. Schumm's (2006: 530) understanding of scaffolding is similar, but not equal to the ZPD: 'providing support for students in their language, and then gradually diminishing the support as students become more independent.' This support has been highlighted in work by Nassaji and Swain (2000) and termed 'negotiated help', i.e., structured scaffolding in regard to the ZPD. They have investigated the effect of random help and negotiated help on the learning of English articles and have found that the ZPD student (who was receiving negotiated help) outperformed the non-ZPD student (who received random help).

Krashen's *i+1* refers to the idea that learners can progress only if they are exposed to input which is just slightly beyond their current developmental level. Determining this for any given learner in advance is neither possible nor predictable. On the other hand, within the ZPD, development for any given learner *can* be predicted on the basis of how he or she responds to the process of mediation. Moreover, Krashen's *i+1* is in line with the language acquisition device (LAD) that is thought to be equal for all learners. In contrast, the development of any learner within the ZPD depends on the type of mediation happening, changes in that mediation and the negotiations between the expert and the novice as well as their quality.

The Socio-Cultural Theory does have some limitations, and one of its weaknesses is that related research as observed L2 use rather L2 acquisition. In addition, there remains a lack of clarity about the type of speech learners are producing or are being offered within the ZPD. Language development has also been linked to other variables, such as the extent to which learners distance from, integrate in or accommodate themselves to the target culture. These observations have been elaborated in Schumann's Acculturation Model and Giles' Accommodation Theory.

The Acculturation Model (Schumann 1978) refers to the assimilation of the cultural traits of the target group by learners. According to this theory,

SLA will be possible only if learners are able to acculturate. Some of the variables inherent to this model are social distance or dominance (referring to the dominance of the group, i.e. if the L1 group is more dominant than the L2, acculturation is more likely to happen), psychological distance (referring to the individual's inner affinity with the target language group) and integration (the extent, will and engagement one individual takes to integrate into the community of the dominant group and to adopt the norms of that group). There is evidence for and against this model. Criticism focuses primarily on the argument that strong causal relationships between social and psychological distance and language learning cannot be established because such variables cannot be said to facilitate learning.

Howard Giles' Accommodation Theory (or Speech Accommodation Theory) shares several theories with the Acculturation Model, but it also has several other significantly different aspects. For Giles, motivation levels reflect how individual learners will define themselves and as a consequence how they change, adjust and accommodate their speech. The theory observes how speech patterns converge or diverge within different social interactions and group constellations. Central to this framework is the notion that speakers are motivated to adjust their speech when interacting with each other. They mainly accommodate their speech when they desire social approval and/or high levels of communicational efficiency. Success will depend on the learners' individual differences and environmental factors as well as each speaker's available language repertoire.

SLA extended: communicating in a world with bilinguals, heritage and multilingual speakers

Given the mobility and migration so common today, as well as economic, trade, cultural, educational and other kinds of encounters – individuals pursue their goals and exchange information by communicating both face-to-face and online in many international settings. These situations often require interlocutors to use a commonly shared or widely understood language, even if it is not their mother tongue. Such a helpful tool is called a 'lingua franca' (Jenkins 2015, Seidlhofer 2011).

English is a widely used lingua franca. According to 2012 Eurobarometer 386, it is by far the language that most Europeans are likely to speak as their first (that is, most fluent) foreign language (32 per cent) (Eurobarometer 386: 20). Speakers might use the lingua franca in different ways depending on the various linguistic practices they have been exercising previously, different norms and the various transfer effects (such as typographical differences) linked to their first languages. These transfer effects are evident in various linguistic domains, such as pronunciation, syntax and/or lexis. The uses of the common language among individuals of various backgrounds are a perfect proof of the cultural diversity inherent in the multilingual world.

Creating and understanding multilingual interactions has become a necessity, bilingualism a fact and monolingualism a rarity. It is important to provide a definition or explanation of these terms, although existing definitions are inconsistent and problematic and fields of bilingual, heritage and multilingual acquisition are broad and complex. This section does not attempt in any way to offer a comprehensive overview of studies and/or recent findings from these fields, but merely attempts to distinguish between them in a general sense.

One of the most well-known and widely used definitions for a *bilingual* person was put forward by Grosjean (1982, 1992), who argues that each bilingual individual functions independently by using two languages and that he or she is not to be understood as an individual who has compiled the two languages as two separate stores. A bilingual person is thus a unique speaker of two languages and integrates knowledge of and from both languages in their everyday communication. According to De Houwer (1995) and Deuchar and Quay (2000), simultaneous bilingualism is the result of children being regularly addressed in two spoken languages from before the age of two, with the acquisition processes continuing up to the final stages of language development. In such cases, both languages are acquired as first languages. This implies the degree of bilingualism, i.e. the proficiency as measured linguistically. For Valdés (2001), the term 'bilingual' should not be limited to just the use of two languages on a daily basis, but rather can also refer to the 'skilled superior use of both languages at the level of the educated native speaker' (Valdés 2001: 40). However, she goes on to state that the process of bilingual acquisition is to be observed as a continuum, as a process and as a product of language learning. In this sense, it is worth mentioning that there is a difference between L2 learners and bilinguals.

Most SLA researchers understand under the term 'bilingual speaker' an individual who has acquired native-speaker competence in a second language, i.e. has undergone a successful SLA process. Regardless of proficiency levels and the onset (i.e. the starting point when learners are being exposed to the new language) of the acquisition in bilinguals, variables such as cognitive effort, inhibitory control, lexical inhibition etc. (Schwieter 2010, 2013 and 2015) also play an important role in the degree of bilingualism attained. A very useful illustration of various types of bilingualism has been compiled by Li Wei (Wei 2000: 6–7). Bilinguals have a number of advantages over monolinguals, including those that are communicative (e.g. greater sensitivity to communication needs of the others), cultural (e.g. more tolerance for other cultures) and cognitive (e.g. divergent and creative thinking, metalinguistic awareness, judgment abilities in term of grammatical accuracy etc.) (cf. Gass *et al.* 2013). These advantages need to be taken into consideration when designing modules and planning actions as part of bilingual education programmes (for more information, see Piske 2013).

Another type of learners, often considered as simultaneously similar to and different from bilinguals, are the *heritage language speakers*. According to Valdés, 'in recent years, the term heritage language has been used broadly to refer to non-societal and non-majority languages spoken by groups often known as linguistic minorities' (Valdés 2005: 411). In defining or researching heritage language learners, it is important to consider variables such as exposure to, and use of, the heritage language in childhood. It is also crucial to highlight that the dominant and primary language in which heritage learners are proficient, and of which they are native speakers, is not the heritage language but rather the language of the community in which they are living. Similarly, there is a difference between language-learning for heritage and non-heritage language students. Oral skills differentiate heritage language-learners from L2 learners in that that the former are better than the latter, but when it comes to written skills, L2 classroom learners have the advantage – probably as the result of classroom learning's focus on instructed learning, in which grammatical accuracy and written skills are usually fostered. The regular use (and learning) of more than two languages has been referred to as *multilingualism* (e.g. Hufeisen 1998). Providing a clear-cut definition for this term seems to be the most challenging task for research on language acquisition beyond a second language. That difficulty arises as a result of the multifaceted nature of a term that has been studied within different frameworks and fields, from traditional, functional, and sociolinguistic to educational. It is certain that more than two languages will be involved in any kind of definition, but what remains vague are the other defining descriptors, starting from whether it is just familiarity with the languages, their regular use or mastery of them. On the individual level, 'multilingualism' is generally understood as the speaker's ability to use two or more languages (see Chapter 2 for information on third-language acquisition).

Nowadays, with the spread of English and globalization, individuals do become multilingual, develop proficiencies in various languages and communicate effectively. With this in mind, the long-term objective of the European Union is that every citizen should have practical skills in at least two foreign languages. This goal has already been reached by some European citizens, as the Eurobarometer Survey has revealed. For example, just over half of Europeans (54 per cent) are able to hold a conversation in at least one language other than their first language, while a quarter (25 per cent) are able to speak at least two additional languages and one in ten (10 per cent) are conversant in at least three. Almost all respondents from the following countries are able to speak at least one language in addition to their mother tongue: Luxembourg (98 per cent), Latvia (95 per cent), the Netherlands (94 per cent), Malta (93 per cent), Slovenia and Lithuania (92 per cent respectively), and Sweden (91 per cent).

Such developments might lead us to question whether existing models of SLA have the capacity to explain the multilingual practices, the competences of multilingual individuals and their goals. In terms of the mastery of a foreign language, multilingual individuals' goals differ from those of learners who only speak one foreign language. The former do not aim to master a language in all its functions, for all purposes and in all contexts. Instead, they adopt the language functions required for the purposes that they find useful and for specific contexts only. In this way, it seems that they build a repertoire of certain competences needed for communication, rather than a total competence in just one individual foreign language. Even their aims are different from those of people just starting out on the process of learning their first foreign language. Multilingual speakers are not aiming at reaching a native-speaker level and thus it would be pointless to measure their proficiency in a certain language against that of a native speaker of the same language. Due to the variety of language constellations inherent in the repertoires of multilingual individuals and the different interactions they are involved in on a daily basis, various acquisition paths and characteristics emerge among multilingual individuals. Hence, we can say that the acquisition paths, rates and outcomes among multilingual speakers are very unpredictable in terms of context and variables.

Real-world applications

The construct of communicative competence clearly gives us valuable insights into the importance of each of its components. Teachers of foreign languages should take into consideration each of these and then employ them appropriately in their classroom methods and materials. Language-teaching methodologies should help learners to reach communicative competence and function appropriately in order to be of use in international communicative situations.

In order to achieve a successful intercultural communication, L2 learners need to acquire the skills required for that and to develop intercultural communicative competence. This competence will help to interpret others' actions and patterns of thinking, will enable them to behave appropriately (and flexibly) when confronted with actions, attitudes and expectations different from their own. Fostering intercultural communicative competence means focusing on both knowledge of the home and target language culture as well as dialects, cross-cultural awareness and paralinguistic signs, such as body language (gestures, touching, silence, pausing etc.).

The role of the teachers in the foreign language learning classroom should be to make learners aware of cultural differences and similarities, as well as to foster the overall communicative competence across the four skills of speaking, writing, reading and listening and to recognize intercultural competence as an inherent part of communicative competence. Learners should be encouraged to work collaboratively. Teachers should provide learners with relevant cultural topics, encourage learners to collect materials on the cultural topics, to broaden their intercultural knowledge and to work collaboratively by reflecting within a cross-cultural discussion platform. Today's students often have broad cultural perspectives as well as different heritage, values, family circumstances and language backgrounds, and teachers need to be aware of these and take care to address that fundamental diversity in the classroom.

The importance of functionalism and its implications for the teaching of an L2 is rooted in the benefits of communication activities. Interactions should be promoted for a meaningful purpose: functional communication activities could involve playing spot the difference with a set of pictures, or filling in the missing feature on a map; social communication activities could involve discussion sessions, debates, dialogues, role plays etc. The focus of functional communication activities is the facilitation of the communication process between the interlocutors rather than mastery of a certain language form. Hence, learners' autonomy and self-monitoring are encouraged. Although functionalism has been criticized for ignoring grammatical errors in its relentless focus on communication accuracy, several strengths have also been identified.

The focus on acquiring communicative competence is one of this approach's main highlights. The fact that the learners are allowed to employ/ use within communicative situation without any pressure and stress is said to enhance their autonomy and to promote self-monitoring. One pedagogical approach in line with the central idea of functionalism is the Task-Based Language Teaching Approach, in which learners engage actively in communication with the aim to fulfil a meaningful task or goal. Hence, language is used as a tool to accomplish the task, which could be along the lines of learners being asked to order food in a restaurant, design a booklet for tourists, make a phone call to find out about certain information needed, etc. In communicative activities such as these, the roles of the learners and the teacher are clearly distinguishable. According to this approach, learners must master the functional processes in communication rather than pay special attention to grammatical forms. Grammar is not necessarily presented in an isolated way, i.e. before the communicative task, nor in an integrated way, i.e. within the communication task. Learners are required to negotiate within groups as part of classroom activities and to accomplish the given meaningful task. Teachers, on the other hand, are facilitators of communicative situations, processes and activities in the classroom, and act as analysts, advisors, guides and group managers.

When applied to learner–teacher interactions, the SCT implies certain tasks for both sides. Can you think of what both parties need to do?

The learner needs:	The teacher needs:

In such contexts, the teacher's role as guide acquires an even greater significance. The Socio-Cultural Theory emphasizes meaningful interaction as the greatest motivating factor in second language learning. Implications deriving from the SCT that refer to the language classroom include aspects of bilingual instruction, fostering of pragmatic skills, inclusion and instruction tailored to personal needs as well as to the changing role of the teacher. In Vygotsky's view, the learning of an L2 has its foundation in the knowledge of one's L1. Furthermore, he also acknowledges that the learning of an L2 depends on the semantic system developed during the acquisition of the L1. The importance of diverse speech modes and genres is an aspect he has discovered and supported. Teachers should help learners become aware of when to use what language depending on the context and purpose of the interlocutors and the communicative situation. According to the precepts of the SCT, the collective experiences gathered through social interaction with peers mediate the inner development of the individual. As a result, Vygotsky objected to the grouping of children according to similarity of knowledge/ skill, because it limits their potential. Teachers should not aim to provide a non-challenging atmosphere without any challenges, but rather offer learners the opportunity to experience diverse types of interaction that enable them to realize their potential. Doing so also entails a clear consideration of one's own needs and interests. Vygotsky sees this as a fundamental principle of education. According to him, meaningful instruction can happen only if the instructional content addresses learners' needs and interests, and if it mirrors their everyday lives in the real world.

Following on from the ZPD, Dynamic Assessment is a powerful framework for assessment and teaching aimed at diagnosing and promoting learning development. Developed and found useful by a variety of educationalists, the main idea of Dynamic Assessment is that teachers should move from focusing on correction to acknowledging the importance of the processes underlying that performance, with the overall goal of providing a clear and more accurate picture of learners' abilities. Dynamic Assessment also offers valuable insights into how teachers can approach the process of task design, namely that activities need to be sufficiently challenging and that learners should not be able to complete them without the mediation offered by a teacher in a carefully prepared context. Although many teachers practise different types of scaffolding, not all of them necessarily take account of the varying degrees of guidance or help which may have different impacts on SLA outcomes.

The implications of the concepts of ZPD and assisted performance teach us that very sensitive correction is needed when assisting second language learners in their development. A correction should at first entail implicit feedback followed by a careful progression of explicit correction that involves more details and explanations. In addition, a thorough examination of learners' progress and abilities is needed in order to be able to assess the degree, amount and type of correction and assistance each person needs. Insights such as these are important for the idea of integrating individually tailored teaching according to learners' needs and the continuous assessment of their emerging abilities.

The decision about when to introduce a certain grammatical form will depend on the approach one supports. An interesting comparison of the differences between a grammatical and a functional syllabus can be seen through an example of the modal *would*. If a grammatical syllabus is followed, *would* would appear in later stages as it is relatively complex, especially in combination with conditionals (e.g. *If I were rich, I would travel around the world for a year*). In a functional syllabus, however, *would* would be introduced at an early stage, because it has a great communicative value even for beginner learners of English.

Weaknesses have been identified in functional approaches and their link to language teaching. For example, it is not easy to decide which different functions to introduce and when; for example, is it more important to be polite, to complain or to apologize? Different levels of formality and the expression of basic functions are also problematic. For example, requests can be made in different ways by using different structures '*Can I . . .?*' versus '*Would you mind if I . . .?*'.

Last but not least, there should be no doubt that the functional approach has influenced the development of language-teaching methodology to some extent. Most new coursebooks contain a functions section alongside the grammatical sections and provide learners with useful expressions for communication. The introduction of structures with high communicative values even at the beginning stages of language acquisition, in comparison to a mere introduction of the present simple of the verb '*to be*' in all its forms, has further advanced the idea that communicative language teaching lies at the core of a successful acquisition process, in which the structures that are needed and useful for actual communication are presented.

The reality of today's communicative situations helps us to understand the world as a multilingual place in which speaking more than two languages has become the norm rather than the exception. Accordingly, teachers are faced with situations in which they must deal with several first languages in one mixed classroom. They are, however, often not provided with any institutional support in these scenarios and must find their own individual (and creative) solutions. In fact, both teachers and researchers face similar challenges when dealing with multilingual individuals. As a result, several questions have emerged:

- How do multilingual individuals deal with the existing resources in their language repertoire?
- Are they able to establish synergies among their languages and extract new information from the target language through analogy?
- What do they transfer into their target language across the different linguistic domains?
- Do they develop extraordinary characteristics (increased working memory capacity, reasoning abilities) that distinguish them from other foreign language-learners as a result of increased language-learning experiences or due to other factors?

- Do they differ in the use of language learning strategies and if yes, how?

- Do they process input in the target language differently from those who only speak their L1s and learn a first foreign language?

- Do they become more flexible, more tolerant and/or more creative as a result of the mediating role they take and exercise when dealing with more than one language regularly?

- Are they better language-learners? If yes, why? If not, why not?

- What can teachers do once they know the answers to these questions?

- What changes will need to be made by teachers in terms of differentiating appropriately and reasonably in the choice of materials, in the delivery of instructional content, choice of methods and approaches in teaching, group constellations, in their facilitating, mediating and guiding roles and in providing input?

Only good action-research can offer answers to these questions. In the meantime, we can all strive to become efficient multilingual speakers with high language awareness, intercultural communicative competence and excellent communication skills.

Where to find more about this topic

Bardovi-Harlig, K., and Vellenga, H.E. (2012). The effect of instruction on conventional expressions in L2 pragmatics. *System*, 40, 77–89.

Elsner, D. and Keßler, J.-U. (eds) (2013), *Bilingual Education in Primary School: Aspects of Immersion, CLIL, and Bilingual Modules*. Tübingen: Narr.

Klein, W., and Dimroth, C. (2009). Untutored second language acquisition. In W. C. Ritchie, and T. K. Bhatia (eds), *The New Handbook of Second Language Acquisition* (2nd rev. ed.; pp. 503–522). Bingley: Emerald.

Nassaji, H., and Swain, M. (2000). A Vygotskian perspective on corrective feedback: The effect of random versus negotiated help on the learning of English articles. *Language Awareness*, 9, 34–51.

Schwieter, J. W. (2010). *Cognition and Bilingual Speech: Psycholinguistic Aspects of Language Production, Processing, and Inhibitory Control*. Saarbrücken: Lambert Academic.

Schwieter, J. W. (ed.) (2013) *Innovative Research and Practices in Second Language Acquisition and Bilingualism*. Amsterdam/Philadelphia, PA: John Benjamins Publishing.

Schwieter, J. W. (ed.) (2015). *The Cambridge Handbook of Bilingual Processing*. Cambridge: Cambridge University Press.

What we
know about
SLA

6

Introduction

Research into SLA has laid the groundwork for a number of important discoveries. Despite the fact that research has expanded enormously since SLA was first established as an area of study, there is ongoing debate – and a number of controversies – about some of its key issues. This is partly due to the complexity and the multifaceted nature of the field. Studies on SLA have increased in quantity as researchers have addressed a variety of topics, asked new questions and worked within multiple research methodologies and from a variety of academic disciplines (e.g. linguistics, applied linguistics, psycholinguistics, psychology, and education). As a result of this multidisciplinary work, we are in a better position to argue that learners acquire a second language through a number of interactive factors, namely: exposure to language input; making use of existing knowledge of their native language; and access to universal properties.

What do we know about L1 and L2 acquisition? How does our language system grow? What is the role of implicit and explicit knowledge in SLA? What is the role of input, interaction and output in SLA? How does instruction impact SLA? In this final chapter we provide a concise evaluation of what we know about this topic and highlight the main real-world applications and implications.

An evaluation of what we know

L1 vs L2

One of the key questions in SLA research is to what extent L1 and L2 acquisition is similar or different. To date, scholars' findings have indicated the following:

Similarities

1 Both L1 and L2 learners need input in order to construct a language system. The Monitor Theory argues that the input learners are exposed to must have two requisites to be good input for acquisition: first, it must be understood by learners; and second, it must contain a message and be communicative. The Universal Grammar Theory also highlights the crucial role that input plays in language acquisition. Quantitative and qualitative differences in input are possible reasons for disparities in L1 and L2 success. High-quality linguistic input is essential for successful language acquisition.

2 In the acquisition of both L1 and L2, learners acquire the formal features of the target language in a predictable and natural order. Findings from research into both the acquisition of grammatical morphemes (e.g. inflectional features) in L1 and L2 have indicated that there is a specific and similar order in the acquisition of morphemes in languages. Furthermore, there is a sequence of acquisition for a number of function words in English as an L1 (e.g. nouns, verb inflections, articles). Similarly, L2 learners acquire grammatical features of a target language in a certain order, regardless of their first language or the context in which they acquired them (progressive -*ing* is acquired before regular past tense -*ed*, which is acquired before the third-person -*s*).

3 Both L1 and L2 acquisition follow certain predictable stages. Processability constrains language development in both cases (see the sections on input and output and language growth in Chapters 3 and 4).

4 Acquisition entails certain marked and unmarked features in language. Unmarked features are those that are universal or which are present in most languages and which learners tend to transfer. Marked features are language-specific, and the learner often resists

transferring these. The distinction between marked and unmarked features applies to different level of linguistics analysis. In syntax, for example, the basic word order in sentences containing SVO (subject-verb-object) is very common in languages and therefore considered an unmarked feature. SOV word order, on the other hand, which is present only in certain languages such as Japanese, is considered a marked feature. The research findings show that unmarked features are learned earlier and easier than marked rules in both the L1 and the L2.

Differences

1 The Fundamental Difference Hypothesis supports the view that the process in which children and adults acquire language is fundamentally different. Children have an innate and internal ability to acquire a language system, and this is impervious to external factors. Adults, on the other hand, do not have access to the same innate ability, and they tend to resort to problem-solving skills to learn a language. The Fundamental Difference Hypothesis also suggests that L2 acquisition is influenced by L1 transfer, social-communicative contexts and affective factors such as attitude.

2 L1 and L2 acquisition differs in terms of route and outcome. According to the Critical Period Hypothesis, students who begin learning a new language after a certain age might not be able to master certain linguistic features. Empirical studies have been undertaken to investigate whether or not age affects learning outcomes. Findings are mixed, but it seems that younger learners and adults have neurological, cognitive and psychological differences that come into play in SLA.

Children are usually considered to be better learners than adults. They tend to have fewer inhibitions than adults and have a desire to actively participate in the social life around them, both of which helps them to learn new languages. They do not have analytical skills and tend to process languages generally through sensory experience, and language develops from exposure to simplified and concrete input. By contrast, adult language learners often fail to master language structure. Differences in context between L1 and L2 acquisition plays an important role in the acquisition process. While it is possible to learn an L2 in various contexts, L1 acquisition takes place only in a natural context and in the social group in which the child is growing up and where he or she receives L1 input only.

Can you think of any other similarities and differences
between L1 and L2 acquisition?

1

2

3

Language growth

SLA research has focused a great deal on interlanguage grammatical
development. Interlanguage is systematic (follows certain rules and patterns)
and seems to evolve over the course of stage-like development.

Orders and developmental sequences

1 The consistency of the results obtained in morpheme studies has led
to the view that L2 learners follow an order in the acquisition of
morphemes. SLA seems to progress in uniform stages. They learn
morphological inflections in a consistent order (like L1 learners).
Using English as an example, this would be: present progressive
(*-ing*); prepositions (in, on, etc); plural (*-s*); past irregular;
possessive (*'s*); articles (*a, the*); past regular (*-ed*); regular third-
person singular (*-s*).

2 Processing skills develops following a particular and hierarchical
sequence: First, words access. Words are processed without any
particular grammatical information. Second, category procedure.
Words are accessed and inflections put on them (e.g. number and
gender to nouns, tense to verbs). Learners are able to add the
morpheme *-ed* to the verb *to talk* to mark past tense (*talked*). Third,
phrasal procedure. Inflections are used at phrase-level. Learners can
perform operations such as agreement for number and gender between
adjective and noun within the noun phrase. Fourth, S-procedure. Here,
grammatical information is exchanged across phrase boundaries.
Learners develop competence in exchanging information between
noun phrases and verb phrases, and are able to produce subject–verb

agreement. Fifth, subordinate clause procedure. Information is exchanged across clauses. Learners develop the ability to carry grammatical and semantic information from the main clause to the subordinate clause, as occurs in the use of the subjunctive.

Learners traverse particular stages in the acquisition of structures (see example below on the acquisition of *ser* and *estar* in Spanish).

- Stage 1: no copular verb – *Juan alto*
- Stage 2*:* use of *ser* – *Maria es muy simpatica*
- Stage 3*: estar* + progressive – *Está estudiando*
- Stage 4*: estar* + location – *Están en Madrid*
- Stage 5*: estar* + adjective of condition – *Estoy muy content*

There is a hierarchy of output-processing procedures which means that if L2 learners are at stage 3 of output processing, they have acquired stages 1 and 2, but not necessarily 4 and 5. A basic tenet of the theory is that learners cannot skip stages and therefore instruction cannot teach learners to do something until they are ready to acquire it.

3 Developmental sequences in L2 learners' acquisition of tense and aspect, both of which involve the acquisition of morphological features, have been studied intensively in SLA in more recent years. Studies of the acquisition of tense and aspect lend strong support to the existence of developmental patterns in L2 acquisition (e.g. past > past progressive > present perfect > past perfect).

Can you find an example of orders and sequence of acquisition in a western or non-western language?

Mental representation and language skills

Mental representation is defined as learners' underlying competence or knowledge. It is both implicit and abstract in nature, and skill is the ability to use language in real time (that is, to develop the ability to be accurate and fluent in a target language). Mental representation is characterized by a number of components (e.g., syntax, lexicon, phonology, and universal features) and these interact to yield what we know as language. Mental representation includes both what it is possible and not possible in a target language (see example below):

- Do you know the way to Greenwich?
- *Know you the way to Greenwich?

Implicit vs explicit

Most researchers view SLA as a largely implicit process that is principally guided by the learners' interaction with L2 input. For these researchers, 'attention' is an important construct, but mainly because it promotes understanding of meaning rather than because it facilitates skill-learning. There is a long-standing debate on whether acquisition is an implicit and unconscious process or explicit and conscious.

1 According to the Monitor Theory, explicit learning about an L2 is possible, but this ability remains separate from the underlying competence in the target language that L2 learners come to acquire. The Monitor Theory makes a distinction between two autonomous processes (learning vs acquisition) and argues that there is no interface between the two.

2 From a generative linguistic perspective, L1 and L2 acquisition is an implicit process. Learners acquire linguistic competence through the unconscious acquisition of the target language's grammatical properties. Universal Grammar properties also play a role in the acquisition of implicit knowledge. Learners create an abstract system (mental representation) similar to that of L1 learners: for example, sentences have an underlying hierarchical structure consisting of phrases (e.g. noun phrase, verb phrase, etc.). Learners know that languages are hierarchical and consist of phrases, and such knowledge is 'built' in (implicit) to the universal properties of languages. Mental representation builds up over time as a result of consistent and constant exposure to input data. Input indicates whether there are variations between two languages. For example, English is head-initial ('*John plays the piano*') and Japanese is head-final ('*John the piano plays*'). In order for learners of English to build a system with head-final if they learn Japanese, they need the input they receive to interact with universal properties in their heads.

3 Usage-based approaches suggest that language acquisition is largely implicit and that the majority of human cognitive processing takes

place outside consciousness. Our internal system makes form–meaning mappings and then expands these constructions through exposure to input, generalizations and abstractions. Learners possess a complex network of form–meaning connections (semantic–lexical–formal relationships). They make one form–meaning connection at a time, thereby creating vast and interconnected networks of lexical entries that encode meaning and grammatical information.

4 The Skill Acquisition Theory argues that explicit L2 knowledge, attained through explicit learning, can become implicit L2 knowledge. This is generally achieved through practice in which learners deliberately focus their attention on L2 forms as they encode message meanings, then work towards understanding and internalization. SLA is viewed as a skill, and its acquisition as a linguistic system which is assumed to be built up gradually through processes of attention, conscious awareness and practice.

5 From a neurolinguistics perspective, a distinction is made between procedural and declarative memory. Procedural memory refers to knowledge about a language which is usually implicit and not available for conscious inspection. Declarative memory is about explicit knowledge that learners develop through language instruction. There seems to be no neurological connection between two systems.

Input, interaction and output

The respective roles of input, interaction and output have been investigated in SLA. Input is an essential and vital ingredient for language acquisition and for the development of an implicit and unconscious system. Broadly speaking, there is no theory about or approach to SLA that does not recognize its importance of input. That said, there are questions around the role of input and output, namely: is input alone sufficient for language acquisition? And what is the role of output in SLA?

Input

1 Input is the communicative meaning-based language data that L2 learners hear or read. It plays a key role in acquisition: indeed, successful acquisition requires first and foremost exposure to comprehensible and communicative input. (No successful learner

acquires a language fully without input.) The Monitor Theory suggests that SLA takes place when the learner understands input that contains grammatical forms that are at a higher level than the current state of his or her interlanguage.

2 Despite the fact that input's crucial impact on acquisition, not all the input we hear or read is learned. According to the Input Processing Theory, only part of the input is passed through intake into the developing system and eventually into output by the learner. Input is filtered before universal properties and/or L1 devices might interact with input. Processing acts as a mediator between the input data and the internal mechanisms responsible for further processing and accommodating the information into our internal system. Understanding processing and misprocessing might help us change the way L2 learners process/filter input. Altering processing might enrich learners' intake and affect their developing system in such a way that ultimately there will be an impact on how they produce the L2. Input processing is concerned with the psycholinguistic strategies and mechanisms by which learners derive intake from input. When learners process input, focusing on the form and understanding the message, a form–meaning connection is made. Developing the ability in L2 learners to map one form to one meaning is essential for acquisition. Equally L2 learners must process syntactic structures correctly and avoid misunderstanding the message conveyed in the input language. Learners make use of implicit processing strategies when they process grammar in the input. They tend to fail to make the right connections and this causes delay in acquisition (for example, in the sentence '*Hier, j'ai joué au tennis avec John*', learners would process the temporal adverb before the grammatical item as they both encode the same semantic information).

> Can you provide another example where learners might fail to make a connection between form and meaning?

3 The Interaction Hypothesis also views input as a significant factor in acquisition and one without which learners will be unable to acquire the target language. This theory draws a distinction between interactional and non-interactional input. Interactional input refers

to input received during interaction where there is some kind of communicative exchange involving the learner and at least another person (e.g. conversation, classroom interactions). Non-interactional input occurs as part of non-reciprocal discourse where learners are not part of an interaction (e.g. announcements). In the case of the former, learners have the advantage of being able to negotiate meaning and make some conversational adjustments. This means that conversation and interaction make linguistic features salient to learners and therefore increase their chances of acquisition.

4   There are cases where some forms or structures are more difficult to acquire through positive evidence alone. This is particularly the case of linguistic features that are not part of the Universal Grammar. There are also a number of factors which affect the acquisition of linguistic constructions: frequency and saliency of features in the input; functional interpretations; reliabilities in terms of form–function mappings; redundancy; and communicative value.

> Can you provide an example of a *redundant* and *non-redundant* form in a western or non-western language?

Interaction

Conversational interaction and negotiation can facilitate acquisition. Learners sometimes request clarifications or repetitions if they do not understand the language they are exposed to. In order to facilitate acquisition, someone can ask another person or request the other to modify their utterances or they can modify their own input in order to be understood. In conversations involving non-native speakers (NNS) and native speakers, negotiations are frequent. Learners sometimes request clarifications or repetitions if they do not understand the input they receive. For example, confirmation checks (e.g. *'did you say. . .?'*); comprehension checks (e.g. *'do you understand?'*); and clarification requests (e.g. *'what did you say?'*) are often used by NNS. Negotiation for meaning facilitates acquisition because it connects input and output.

Output

Output is the language that L2 learners produce with communicative intent. The Comprehensible Output Hypothesis suggests that language production (oral and written) can help learners to generate new knowledge and consolidate or modify their existing knowledge. It assigns several roles for output: output practice helps learners to improve fluency; output practice helps learners to check comprehension and linguistic correctness; output practice helps learners to focus on form; output helps learners to realize that their developing system is faulty and therefore notice a gap in their system. Comprehensible input might not be sufficient to develop native-like grammatical competence, however, and thus learners also need exposure to comprehensible output. Learners needs 'pushed output' – speech or writing that will force them to produce language correctly, precisely and appropriately. The ability to produce forms and structures in output does not necessarily mean that forms and structures have been acquired, of course, but output promotes the noticing of linguistic features in the input and conscious awareness of language and language use. It can also provide additional input to learners so that they can consolidate or modify their existing knowledge. Output promotes awareness and interaction with other learners but it might not play a direct role in the creation of the internal linguistic system.

Instruction

What is the role of instruction in SLA? There are two main views: first, instruction has a limited and constrained role; second, instruction might have a beneficial role under certain conditions. These theoretical views are based on the assumption that the route of acquisition cannot be altered. However, instruction might in certain conditions speed up the rate of acquisition and develop greater language proficiency. What are the conditions that might facilitate the speed in which languages are learnt? The first condition is that L2 learners must be exposed to sufficient input. A second condition is that L2 learners must be psycholinguistically ready for instruction to be effective. A third condition is that instruction must take into consideration how L2 learners process the input.

1 The Monitor Theory posits that instruction plays a limited role in SLA. It argues that acquisition is an unconscious and implicit process, and that learners acquire a second language through exposure to comprehensible and meaning-bearing input rather than learning grammar consciously through explicit grammatical rules. In addition to the limited role assigned to grammar instruction, the theory argues

that L2 learners acquire grammatical features (e.g. morphemes) of a target language in a predictable order, regardless of their L1 or the context in which they acquire them.

2 The Processability Theory supports the view that L2 learners acquire single structures in predictable stages. According to this theory, instruction is constrained by these developmental stages, and L2 learners follow a very rigid route in the acquisition of grammatical features which cannot be skipped. If instruction is targeted at grammatical features for which L2 learners are developmentally ready, then instruction can be beneficial in helping them to move faster along their natural route of development. If learners are instructed and they are not ready, however, instruction can be detrimental to acquisition.

3 The Interaction Hypothesis suggests that there is some evidence for the thesis that instruction helps L2 learners to develop a good level of attainment, particularly if opportunities to natural exposure are given. Instruction has a facilitative role when it is used to acquire linguistic features, which are not too far removed from the learner's current level of language development. Instruction might have a facilitative role in helping learners to pay selective attention to form and form–meaning connections in the input.

4 Learners make form–meaning connections from the input they receive as they connect particular meanings to particular forms (grammatical or lexical). For example, they tend to connect a form with its meaning in the input they receive (the morpheme –ed on the end of the verb in English refers to an event in the past). The Input Processing Theory indicates that L2 learners do not necessarily attend to form and meaning simultaneously with the input they receive. Therefore, they must be trained on how to process input more effectively and efficiently so that they are in a better position to process grammatical forms and connect them with their meanings.

Activity

What is your view on the following statements?

Do you agree or disagree? Please explain why.

1 Grammar should be taught (explaining rules) and learners should practise grammar mechanically (drills).

    Agree   Disagree

2 Errors should be corrected.

    Agree   Disagree

3. Simple language structures should be learned before complex ones.

    Agree   Disagree

4 Communication can be defined as the expression, interpretation and negotiation of meaning.

    Agree   Disagree

5 Language classrooms should be more input-rich.

    Agree   Disagree

6 Grammar should move from input to output practice.

    Agree   Disagree

7 Language classrooms should provide learners with opportunities to interact and to negotiate meaning.

    Agree   Disagree

8. Output practice should focus on skills.

    Agree   Disagree

Instruction might be more facilitative if it were less about the teaching of rules and more about exposure to forms. Similarly it might have a facilitative role if it were less concerned with manipulating output and more with processing input. The focus of instruction should be on processing and not on production, at least at the beginning of acquisition.

Real-world applications

Research into SLA has focused on several issues concerning the learner and the learning processes, and the resulting theories have clear implications for teachers and students alike. So what are the main real-world applications of second-language theory and second-language research?

Grammar instruction

Over the last thirty years, empirical research on the effects of grammar instruction has offered clear insights on how learners process and acquire grammar. Findings from these studies have caused a dramatic shift from traditional grammar-oriented approaches to more communicative grammar-oriented approaches. In traditional instruction, grammar is taught through paradigmatic explanations of the grammatical rules followed by mechanical practice (drills) to ensure learners develop accuracy in using the target feature. Yet classroom-based research in SLA has demonstrated that traditional instruction does not foster acquisition. The most important issue for instructors is not whether or not they should teach grammar at all, but rather how and what they should teach.

Grammar instruction should be incorporated in a more communicative framework of language teaching by means of tasks that enhance the grammatical features in the input. The more researchers learn about what learners do with input and how they do it, the closer they come to understanding the possibilities of instructional effects. Grammar instruction should aim at manipulating the input L2 learners receive by enhancing the grammar in the text. For example, related tasks could make use of typographical cues such as bolding and italics to draw learners' attention (noticing) to grammatical forms and provide them with communicative input. The main guidelines for developing textual enhancement tasks are:

- establish a goal;
- choose an appropriate form;
- choose a text that it is appropriate to the level;
- consider the frequency of exposure;
- consider how you draw learners' attention;
- keep meaning in focus.

Structured input tasks enhance form–meaning relationships and make one form more salient in the input. Despite the different options available for teaching grammar, it must be emphasized that effective types of grammar instruction share a common and essential ingredient: input. Instructors should ensure that input is manipulated so as to facilitate input processing and grammar acquisition. Learners should be encouraged to make accurate form–meaning mappings. Grammar tasks should focus on both form and meaning and grammar output-based practice ought to follow input-based practice. See the guidelines below for developing structured input tasks:

- present one thing at a time;
- keep the meaning in focus;

- move from sentences to connected discourse;
- use both oral and written input;
- have learners do something with the input;
- keep the learners' processing strategies in mind.

While structured input tasks help learners make better form–meaning connections and facilitate language development, the question is: how do we access the information we need for speech production? In short, we need to stimulate communicative language use. Learners must be encouraged to make use of a particular target feature in a specific communicative context. They need to express a particular meaning by retrieving a particular structure or word. Structured output tasks help learners to develop the ability to string structures and words together. These tasks require the exchange of previously unknown information as learners access a particular form or structure to express meaning. See below guidelines to develop structured output tasks:

- present one thing at a time;
- keep the meaning in focus;
- move from sentences to connected discourse;
- use both oral and written output;
- others must respond to the content of the output;
- the learner must have some knowledge of the form or structure.

Grammar instruction should move from input to output tasks (see Table 6.1, which contains a list of possible features that teachers can use to develop structured input and structured output tasks).

Error correction

The role of error correction in SLA has been widely debated, spawning a great deal of theoretical and empirical research, but its role remains unclear. Research on this issue has attempted to prove that error correction is both effective and necessary. Explicit error correction provides learners with a meta-linguistic explanation about the error made. While this kind of direct error correction might have a temporary effect (in improving performance), it does little good in the long run and does change L2 learners' underlying implicit system. Implicit error correction indirectly and incidentally informs learners of their non-target-like use of certain linguistic features. Recasts (reformulating the utterance with the correct form), confirmation checks, clarification requests, and even paralinguistic signs such as facial expressions can all constitute indirect correction techniques. Implicit error correction

Table 6.1 Use of structured input and structured output tasks

Example of grammatical features/forms affected by Principle 1 and sub-principles	Example of grammatical features affected by Principle 2
Tense markers when adverbials time are present	Word order
Subject–verb agreement when explicit subjects are present	Passive constructions
	Case marker
Aspectual markers when adverbials of aspect are present	Object pronouns
	Causative form
Mood when expression of uncertainty or emotion are present	
Subjunctive	
Adjective agreement (Italian)	
Case markers (German)	
Negation with *avoir* (French)	
Third-person singular *-s* marker	
Certain prepositions	

aims at helping learners to detect a discrepancy between their utterance and the target language. For implicit corrective feedback, one fundamental question is: how do such indirect signals help learners recognize a discrepancy? Two hypotheses have been proposed: first, implicit error correction offers the opportunity to make a comparison; second, the output driven by the correction can stimulate learners to notice the gap.

Indirect error correction techniques can be further classified into two types: recast and repair. Recast provides the correct form immediately after learner errors (see example below).

- NNS: I go holiday in Italy.
- NS: You go on holiday to Rome?
- NNS: Yes, on holiday to Rome.
- NS: Wow, how nice.

Repair techniques such as clarification requests (e.g. *'What did you say?'*, *'Do you mean. . .?'*) do not provide target-like form but prompt learners to repair their errors by themselves. Empirical support for repair suggests that this kind of error correction can assist learners in actively confronting errors in ways that may lead to revisions of their hypotheses about the target language. Support for recast suggests that it might enable learners to be exposed to target forms and elicit repetition, and this repetition may, in turn, enhance salience. Effective error-correction techniques are the ones that seem to produce student-generated repairs. Language instructors should encourage learners to self-correct and provide appropriate cues for the learner to self-repair.

Rule-based instruction

Instructors generally believe that learning rules causes the acquisition of a target language. Yet when we look at the way languages are learned, we begin to ask ourselves whether or not providing rules helps at all. SLA requires L2 learners to be exposed to comprehensible and meaningful input (explicit information about a target language is not input for acquisition). Instructed SLA research has shown that learning rules is not what makes the difference; Acquisition is not driven by explicit rules but mainly by interaction of language universal properties with input data. Providing explicit information and giving rules might help in terms of proving L2 learners with the opportunity to monitor their speech to perform certain tasks, but the internal developing system is built up via the regular channels of acquisition and it is not affected by learning the explicit rules of a target language. SLA is complex and consists of various processes acting sometime on different data. If we take the English third-person singular -s, it is understood that it is an easy rule to learn explicitly, but at the same time, research has indicated that L2 learners find it very difficult to acquire this rule and find it hard to produce it. The explanation is that there are multiple factors which would explain the difficulty in acquiring certain rules. In the case of the third-person -s in English, a combination of factors including redundancy and the communicative value of this rule and other factors (e.g. strategies used by L2 learners to process words and forms in the input) would make this rule challenging to process and acquire.

The role of communication and the centrality of meaning

The concept of communication is at the heart of language acquisition. Communicative language ability develops as learners engage in communication, which can be defined as the expression, interpretation and negotiation of meaning. Mechanical practice does little to foster language development and encourages only a learning-like behaviour. Real communication is about language use in context.

Learners learn to communicate by using language in meaningful contexts and negotiating input, as the example below shows:

NNS: *'Did you have a nice weekend?'*
NNS: *'Hum . . .?'*
NNS: *'Saturday, Sunday . . . did you have fun?'*

Interaction fosters acquisition when a communication problem arises and learners resolve it by working together to negotiate meaning. Features of language are learned if they have been linked to a real-world meaning. Communication is thus not simply a matter of questions and answers but involves expression, interpretation and negotiation of meaning. Tasks that can be used in the classroom to promote effective learning should require L2 learners to comprehend, manipulate and produce the target language as they perform communicative tasks.

Developing effective tasks

Instruction should move from input practice to output practice. As noted above, successful acquisition is intake-dependent and so instructors need to give learners the opportunities to make correct form–meaning connections in the input they are exposed to. Once learners have hopefully internalized forms, made those form–meaning mappings (through structured input activities or other communicative grammar tasks, rather than through drills or pattern practice) and been able to use them, they then need the opportunity to use the target language for communicative purposes.

Oral communicative practice is the antithesis of the oral practice featured widely in traditional textbooks. In these more formal tasks, learners are asked to look at some pictures or a piece of dialogue and then reproduce that dialogue following a specific pattern. Alternatively they might be asked to talk about a topic (e.g. describing a friend or family member, talking about their weekend, etc) without taking into consideration communication's main principles (as noted above, it involves the expression, interpretation and negotiation of meaning in a given context). Oral tasks should be designed to allow language instructors and learners interact with each other by completing a number of communicative tasks. The role of the instructor is to design the oral task and encourage participation and contribution from learners. The learners' role is to share responsibility with each other by completing a number of communicative tasks. By providing a series of tasks to complete we encourage learners to generate information themselves rather than just receiving it. Language instructors should develop oral tasks in which learners are provided with opportunities to speak the target language at all times in a rich environment that contains collaborative work, authentic materials and tasks in which they can share knowledge by interacting with each other. Being able to communicate in a second language clearly and efficiently contributes to how successfully a second language is acquired overall, and it is therefore crucial that language instructors pay greater attention to the development of speaking skills. Rather than leading learners to pure memorization, they should provide them with a stimulating environment where meaningful communication takes place. Tasks that involve exchanging information, identifying gaps in information, and even certain types of role play, for example, can greatly contribute in the communicative skills learners require if they are to acquire a second language. The main guidelines for developing effective speaking tasks are:

- selecting a topic that is familiar, appropriate, interesting and relevant to the real world;
- designing an appropriate purpose for the task;
- clarifying the information source required, i.e. the kind of language, function and grammar needed to complete the task.

Writing is a cognitive process that involves a series of sub-processes. It allows learners to explore, consolidate and develop rhetorical objectives. As with speaking, the main goal of writing is successful communication, but all too often traditional writing tasks do not achieve this. When designing a writing activity for L2 learners, language teachers should encourage learners (via a step-by-step approach) to work together in order to generate content, select a purpose, plan and organize the composition (pre-writing activities) of the piece and eventually review and evaluate the content and form of their composition. Guidelines for developing an effective writing task are:

- generating the initial idea;
- selecting a purpose;
- planning the execution of the task;
- organizing the composition;
- reviewing and evaluating the composition;

When designing a reading comprehension task, we should take into account the processes responsible for reading comprehension and develop a step-by-step approach (pre-reading–reading–post-reading) similar to the one used for writing. The Schema Theory suggests that as learners, our knowledge impacts on how we process and understand new information. The pedagogical implication of this is the understanding that reading is an interactive process between readers and texts and readers must associate elements in a text with their pre-reading knowledge. Reading activities in traditional textbooks consist mainly of two types: translation tasks (reading a passage and translating it); and answering questions about a text. Reading should be viewed as 'reading in another language rather than as an exercise in translation'. The fact that language learners do not necessarily have the verbal virtuosity of a native reader means instructors need to use some strategies to help them. Effective reading and comprehension tasks should take into consideration the need to guide learners in their comprehension of a text. Developing reading comprehension skills involves the interaction of a variety of knowledge sources. In Chapter 6 we proposed an interactive model to develop L2 learners' reading skills. Reading comprehension tasks should be developed in order to stimulate learners' motivation and should have specific communicative purposes and goals. A five-stage approach would be beneficial:

1   the *pre-reading* stage prepares students for reading and activating their background knowledge;

2   the *reading* stage helps learners to read the text and scan for specific information or meanings;

3   the *text-interaction* stage helps to gradually bridge the gap between the text and the reader;

4   the *post-reading* stage checks and verifies learners' comprehension of the text;

5   the *personalization* stage helps learners to exploit the communicative function of the text through the use of various tasks (e.g. solving a problem, creating a poster, applying main concepts to another context, and relating key issues to a different context).

Specific guidelines for second language instructors are as follows:

- pre-reading
- guided interaction
- assimilation
- personalization

In order to develop learners' aural skills, instructors should provide tasks which reflect real-world listening situations. Learners should be guided in terms of what meanings they should expect from the passage. At the same time, learners must be able to take responsibility for extracting the main content/ information from the text. As discussed above, the role of comprehensible input and conversational interaction has assumed greater importance in second language teaching as learners benefit a great deal from exposure to comprehensible input, conversational interaction and opportunities for negotiation of meaning.

Listening is not just a bottom-up process where learners hear sounds and need to decode them, but also a top-down process where learners reconstruct the speaker's original meaning by using incoming sounds as clues. In this reconstruction process, the listener uses prior knowledge of the context and situation within which the aural exercise takes place to make sense of what he or she hears. Listeners use a series of mental processes as well as their prior knowledge to understand and interpret what they hear. Listening is a very active skill given that learners are engaged in a variety of processes simultaneously while they are exposed to aural stimuli. The challenge is to develop listening tasks that will stimulate the development of listening skills while equipping learners with listening strategies. Suggested guidelines include:

- exposing listeners to comprehensible input;
- using the target language to conduct classroom business;
- allowing learners to nominate topics and structure the discourse. They are much more likely to get involved and become active listeners and participants as a result;
- developing listening tasks with specific communicative purposes
- responding to the learner as a listener, not an instructor;
- providing some good listening strategies to learners. In addition to simply allowing more opportunities for collaborative listening, instructors can also point out to learners typical listening gambits for signalling non-understanding, confirmation, and so forth.

A three-stage approach should be followed by instructors (pre-listening–listening–post listening).

In the pre-listening stage, language instructors should set the context, create motivation and activate learners' prior knowledge through cooperative learning tasks (e.g. brainstorming, think-pair-share). Pre-listening tasks include vocabulary learning and/or identifying key ideas contained in the upcoming input.

In the listening stage, learners will need to listen for the main ideas in the audio extract in order to establish the context and transfer information. Learners should be exposed to bottom-up listening tasks (e.g. word–sentence recognition, listening for different morphological endings), top-down tasks (e.g. identifying the topic, understanding the meaning of sentences) and interactive tasks (e.g. listening to a list and categorizing the words, following directions). Main listening tasks can include guided note-taking, or completing a picture or schematic diagram or table.

Finally, in the post-listening stage, learners examine functional language and infer the meaning of vocabulary (e.g. guessing the meaning of unknown vocabulary, analyzing how successful communication has been in the script, and brainstorming alternative ways of expression). Tasks might include additional reading, writing, speaking, and interaction activities.

Teaching methodologies

Language specialists are always interested in finding out the best way to teach languages. In the last forty years we have witnessed a variety of methods in language teaching (e.g. Grammar-Translation, the Natural Approach, Communicative Language Teaching, and Task-Based Language Teaching). There is, however, no 'right' method for teaching languages. Practitioners should instead talk about principled and evidence-based approaches to language teaching which should be drawn from principles, theories and research in second language acquisition, language use and communication. Language instructors are encouraged to take suggestions from a variety of sources when it comes to pedagogical issues, as long as what they choose is guided and informed by theory and empirical research in language learning and teaching. In this book, we have made the case for a learner-centred type of instruction, where L2 learners engage in communicative and effective tasks that involve group work and interaction with other learners. A teaching environment in which learners are exposed to tasks geared to a specific purpose and where the instructor is in the position to give the students many opportunities for spontaneous production, interaction and negotiation of meaning should be achieved. Comprehensible input is required, as are opportunities for learners to interact with their peers. We advocate a different role for the language instructor to the traditional norm, and suggest one that creates the opportunities and classroom conditions required for L2 learners to co-participate and take responsibility for their learning. In this new environment, learning can take place naturally and teaching can be effective. Meaning is emphasized over form and correction kept to a minimum, so that students express themselves without pressure and self-repair. Comprehensible, simplified and message-based input is provided through the use of contextual props, cues, and gestures rather than structural grading. A variety of tasks and discourse types are introduced by role-playing, stories and authentic materials. L2 learners are exposed to tasks in which they engage in the interpretation, expression and negotiation of meaning.

In this new and effective teaching and learning environment, teachers' main aim should be to determine each lesson's principal goals. In traditional instruction, these goals are often reduced to simply completing a chapter in a textbook or covering a particular form, set of vocabulary or a grammatical structure. In a principled and evidence-based approach to language teaching, however, lesson goals should be constructed in such a way that encompasses

Figure 6.1 Task and sub-tasks required to achieve a proficiency goal

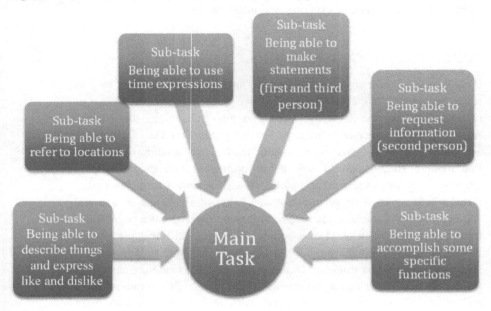

all the vocabulary, grammar, and language functions that learners need to grasp in order to accomplish a particular task. Let's assume that our proficiency goal is 'to talk about how you spent your holiday'. Instructors would need to develop sub-tasks for learners that have the necessary grammar, vocabulary language functions to achieve the proficiency goal set (see Figure 6.1).

Concluding remarks

Research and theories in SLA emphasize the complexity of acquisition processes. They have provided the following insights into language acquisition:

1 Acquisition is largely implicit. In the view of most researchers, acquisition of a second language is primarily a matter of developing implicit knowledge. Mental representation is built over time and requires input and interaction with universal language principles.

2 Acquisition is constrained by orders and sequences. Internal and implicit processes responsible for language acquisition are similar

regardless of the learners' first language. Learners process grammar by following a natural order and a specific sequence (i.e. they master different grammatical structures in a relatively fixed and universal order and they pass through a sequence of stages of learning en route to mastering each structure).

3 Acquisition is input-dependent. L2 learners require extensive second language input exposure to build their internal new linguistic systems. Input needs to be easily comprehensible and message-oriented if it is to be processed effectively by learners. Research into SLA has shown that learners focus primarily on meaning when they process elements of the new language. Input might trigger other universal language properties.

4 Acquisition is process-dependent. It requires learners to make form–function connections (i.e. the relation between a particular form and its meaning/s).

5 Acquisition requires opportunities for output practice. Production serves to generate better input through the feedback that learners' efforts at production elicit. Interaction with other speakers is also a contributing factor in promoting acquisition. However, output processing is constrained. There is an implicational hierarchy of output processing procedures which L2 learners cannot skip.

Table 6.2 Summary of SLA theories

SUMMARY	Input	Output and Interaction	Instruction	Feedback / Error Treatment
UG Theory	Input is the evidence (positive or negative) out of which the learner constructs knowledge of language.	Mainly in the form of grammaticality judgments.	• There is no need to teach principles because they are universal and exist in all languages. • Vocabulary items and how they occur in sentences do need to be taught.	/

continued

Table 6.2 Continued

SUMMARY	Input	Output and Interaction	Instruction	Feedback / Error Treatment
Monitor Theory	• Input should be comprehensible. • Input is beneficial if it is one stage beyond the learner's current stage ($i+1$).	• L2 learner's output mentioned only in reference to a comparison with an ideal native speaker's competence and performance. • Interaction with native speakers seen as beneficial.	• Distinction is made between 'learning' and 'acquisition' and there is no interface between them. • SLA is implicit and instruction plays a limited role.	/
The Interaction Hypothesis	Interactional input is a significant factor for acquisition.	Conversation and interaction make linguistic features salient to learners and therefore increase chances of acquisition.	/	Through negotiation of meaning and conversational adjustments.
The Comprehensible Output Hypothesis	Input is needed for the meta-linguistic function of output, i.e. helping learners to think about language and to compare it.	Interaction is important for learners to notice the gap between what they want to say and what they actually can say.	/	Only on the individual level, i.e. through self-correction, analysis of language, noticing gaps, making repairs, testing hypotheses and monitoring.
Processability Theory	Input will be beneficial only if it is close to the learner's developmental stage, otherwise it can be detrimental.	The role of output is acknowledged in the sense that by it the teacher has the opportunity to determine the developmental stages of his/her learners.	• Not everything that is taught is necessarily also learnable. • Learners need to be developmentally ready.	A differentiation between developmental and variational errors has to be made.

			• Instruction is limited and constrained by L2 learners' readiness to acquire a particular structure. • Instruction cannot change the developmental route, but it can speed up the acquisition process.	
Input Processing	• Input is crucial. • Input needs to be comprehensible, i.e. it may have to be manipulated in some cases.	• Input processing (i.e. correct form–meaning mapping) is a pre-requisite for correct output. • Interaction incorporated as part of the exchange of information elements of the structured-input activities (Processing Instruction – product of IP).	• Structured-input activities bring about correct form–meaning mappings. • Explicit information does not matter in the long run, as SLA is implicit.	Implicit short feedback aimed at instilling the proper processing strategies favoured over explicit, as the former fosters acquisition in the long run.
Procedural and declarative model	Input frequencies affect the procedural system.	Meaningful practice affects the procedural system.	/	/
Skill Acquisition Theory	Important only insofar as learners will have opportunities to repeat communication means without focus on form.	• Repeated practice brings about the transformation of declarative into procedural knowledge. • Language seen as any other "skill" that can be learned through practice.	Not clear how teachers can help learners to transfer from declarative to procedural knowledge within various contexts.	• Learners need to receive error correction. • Explicit feedback is crucial.

continued

Table 6.2 Continued

SUMMARY	Input	Output and Interaction	Instruction	Feedback / Error Treatment
Usage-based Theory	The frequent input matters.	The structures of language emerge as a result of interrelated patterns of experience, social interaction and cognitive processes.	• The teacher needs to ensure that the presented input is highly frequent. • The teacher should make use of the categorization options and present language in the form of chunks.	No feedback, inductive-discovery based learning.
Functionalist Theories	• Focus is primarily on input used for communication purposes, i.e. interactional. • More important to use input from and for communication than to master certain language forms.	• Main focus on interaction and function. • Focus on meaningful communicative activities. • Fostering communicative competence.	• The teachers need to create/facilitate and guide meaningful communicative activities. • Fulfilling the task matters, i.e. focus on language functions rather than forms.	Through negotiation of meaning and conversational adjustments.
Socio-cultural Theories	Input is important when it comes within interaction.	L2s can be acquired mainly through social interaction through the support of an expert.	The teachers should provide activities that will allow students to socialize and interact.	• The role of corrective feedback seen as the most influential aspect. • Progression from implicit to explicit feedback.

How is SLA linked to the real world? Research and theories in this field of enquiry have important real world implications (see Table 6.2):

a) Instruction needs to be predominantly directed at developing implicit knowledge, taking into consideration the typical orders and stages of learners' development.

b) Instruction needs to provide learners with comprehensible, simplified, modified and message-oriented input.

c) Instruction ought to be less about manipulating output and more about processing input.

d) Instruction should focus on providing opportunities for learners to use language spontaneously and meaningfully. Corrective feedback in the form of recasting could provide more opportunities for input exposure.

e) Instruction should ensure that the amount of error correction is kept to a minimum, and that learners are encouraged to self-repair.

f) Instruction needs to create opportunities for interaction and negotiation of meaning among speakers. Interaction fosters learning when a communication problem arises and learners are engaged in resolving it through interaction and negotiation of meaning.

g) Instruction needs to provide learners with opportunities to focus on grammatical form within a communicative context. Pedagogical interventions that promote learning are the ones who provide a focus on form and a focus on meaning through input manipulations techniques. Grammar instruction can move from structured input to structured output practice.

h) Instruction should ensure that learners are exposed to extensive 'high-quality' input. However, it is also essential that learners are given opportunities for output.

i) Instruction must provide learners with an opportunity to participate in communicative tasks to develop implicit knowledge. Learners need to be involved in a variety of communicative tasks (e.g. storytelling, jigsaws, finding information gaps, problem-solving and collaborative work) which require them to take responsibility in communicating and interacting with other speakers.

j) Instruction should ensure that learners work in pairs or in groups during the completion of a language task. In group work, learners should be encouraged to negotiate meaning, and to use a variety of linguistic forms and functions.

k) Instruction must create opportunities for learners to communicate by performing communicative functions (output). Whenever learners produce language, it should be for the purpose of expressing some kind of meaning.

Where to find more about this topic

Benati, A. (2013). *Issues in Second Language Teaching*. Sheffield: Equinox.

Benati, A., and Lee, J. (2008). *Grammar Acquisition and Processing Instruction*. Clevedon: Multilingual Matters.

Brantmeier, C. (ed.) (2009). *Crossing Languages and Research Methods: Analyses of Adult Foreign Language Reading*. Book series entitled Research in Second Language Learning. Greenwich, CT: Information Age Publishing.

Gass, S., & Selinker, L. (2008). *Second Language Acquisition: An Introductory Course*. New York, Routledge.

Field, J. (2008). *Listening in the Language Classroom*. Cambridge: Cambridge University Press.

Lee, J., and VanPatten, B. (2003). *Making Communicative Classrooms Happen*. New York: McGraw-Hill.

Lightbown, P., and Spada, N. (2008). *How Languages Are Learned*. Oxford: Oxford University Press.

Long, M. (2007). *Problems in SLA*. Mahwah, NJ: Lawrence Erlbaum Associates.

Meisel, J. (2011). *First and Second Language Acquisition*. Cambridge: Cambridge University Press.

Nassaji, H., and Fotos, S. (2011). *Teaching Grammar in Second Language Classrooms*. New York: Routledge.

Robinson, P. (ed.) (2012). *Routledge Encyclopedia of Second Language Acquisition*. New York: Routledge.

Sheen, Y. (2011). *Corrective Feedback, Individual Differences and Second Language Learning*. New York: Springer.

Savignon, S (2005). *Communicative Competence: Theory and Classroom Practice*. New York: McGraw-Hill.

VanPatten, B. (2003). *From Input to Output. A Teacher's Guide to Second Language Acquisition*. New York: McGraw-Hill.

VanPatten, B, and Benati, A. (2015). *Key Terms in Second Language Acquisition*. London: Bloomsbury.

VanPatten, B., and Williams, J. (eds) (2015). *Theories in Second Language Acquisition*. Mahwah, NJ: Lawrence Erlbaum Associates.

Williams, J. (2005). *Teaching Writing in Second and Foreign Language Classrooms* New York: McGraw-Hill.

Wong, W. (2005). *Input Enhancement: From Theory and Research to the Classroom*. New York: McGraw-Hill.

Glossary

access Access is considered to be processes involved in language acquisition and can be described as the ability of learners to express a particular meaning by having access to a form or a structure and stringing them together in a sentence. Learners might or might not have access to linguistic features in order to produce language. The construct of access is also linked to those of accuracy and fluency in a second language. To gain a greater perspective, read VanPatten (2003, Chapter 4).

Accommodation Theory The Accommodation Theory, also known as the Speech Accommodation Theory, observes how speech patterns converge or diverge within different social interactions and group compositions. Central to this framework is the notion that speakers are motivated to adjust their speech when they interact with others. To gain a better understanding of this theory, read Giles and Smith (1979).

Acculturation Model The Acculturation Model was proposed by Schumann (1978) and refers to a process whereby learners assimilate the cultural traits of those speaking their target language. According to this theory, SLA will be possible only if learners are able to acculturate. For more details, read Schumann (1978).

acquisition Acquisition is usually related to the concept of internalizing a language system and to how learners make use of that linguistic system during comprehension and speech production. Researchers have investigated a number of issues to understand how learners process linguistic features in the input, how these features are mentally represented and how they use their internal competence for practical use. See VanPatten and Williams (2015, Chapter 1).

acquisition orders Learners seem to acquire grammar elements in a specific order, both in their L1 and L2. There a number of linguistics and processing factors responsible for this, such as saliency, communicative value, redundancy, frequency and transparency. In English verbal inflections, the following acquisition order has been found: progressive -*ing;* regular past tense; irregular past tense; third-person -*s.* for more information, read Larsen-Freeman and Long (1991, Chapter 4).

adaptive control of thought model This model refers to the interface between declarative and procedural knowledge. It posits that the most proficient learners seem to move from a controlled to a more autonomous stage in the acquisition of a second language. To gain a greater perspective, read Anderson (1993).

age Age is considered one of the major affective factors in SLA research. A great variety of views have been expressed on the correlation between age and ultimate attainment in both children and adults. For more information, read Birdsong (2006).

aptitude Aptitude is generally defined as a number of linguistic abilities (e.g. phonemic, grammatical, memory-related) which might be held co-responsible for language acquisition. See Robinson (2001).

attention Attention is a cognitive process involving learners' ability to select and focus on specific stimuli from the input they are exposed to, while at the same time ignoring others. Capacity, detection and task demands are constructs linked to attention. See Schmidt (2001).

avoidance Avoidance occurs when L2 learners attempt to avoid using difficult structures, which they perceive as such as a result of differences or similarities between their L1 and the target L2. To find more about avoidance, read Schachter (1974).

awareness Awareness is the degree to which language learners are conscious of what they are doing or learning. Learners are considered aware of a given experience if they can: first, show that a change (cognitive or behavioural) has taken place as a result of that experience; second, report that they are aware of what they are experiencing (e.g. they report noticing linguistic features in the input); and third, describe their experience (e.g. verbalize an underlying rule of the L2). To gain a greater perspective on this issue, read Leow (1997).

behaviourism This early theory in the SLA field makes as its fundamental claim that learning is acquisition due to habit-formation. See Skinner (1957).

bilingualism The study of the nature of the knowledge and use of two languages as spoken by one individual. To gain a better perspective on this broad term, read Bhatia and Ritchie (2004).

communicative competence Introduced by Hymes, the original idea behind this concept was that grammatical competence alone is not enough for learners to be able to communicate effectively. The four components of communicative competence are: linguistic, sociolinguistic, discourse and strategic competence. To find more about this term, read Hymes (1972) and Canale (1983).

communication strategies With this term, we refer to the methods used by non-native speakers to convey a meaning using descriptive devices. To find more about communication strategies, read Yule and Tarone (1997).

competence Competence denotes an individual's knowledge of how a language functions, the rules of that language, and what form or structure is appropriate in which context and situation. To understand the whole concept in more depth, read Chomsky (1965).

competition model This offers an explanation for how people come to choose, associate and link appropriate cues when there are multiple cues available. See MacWhinney (2001).

complexity theory Complexity theory is concerned with the behaviour of dynamic systems (non-linear, chaotic, and unpredictable) that change over time. Acquisition is the product of chaos posed to a state of being. It emerges from the interactions of its components. Read Larsen-Freeman (2015, Chapter 12).

connectionism/emergentism Connectionism considers acquisition as the creation of a number of associations between stimuli and responses which increasingly become stronger. This is in contrast with a universal and abstract concept of the internal system and its growth. To gain a greater perspective, read Ellis and Wulff (2015, Chapter 5).

contrastive analysis Contrastive analysis is an approach which attempts to explain possible problems in second language acquisition through the analysis of similarities and differences between L1 and L2. To gain a greater perspective, read Lado (1957).

Critical Period Hypothesis The Critical Period Hypothesis originates from research on L1 acquisition. The basic notion is that although learners are successful in acquiring their first language, the mechanisms used to acquire it are 'turned off' by a certain age. Learners thus do not have access to the same mechanisms when learning a second language once they have reached that age. For more information, read Singleton (2007).

declarative and procedural knowledge Proponents of these concepts argue that learning starts with declarative knowledge but that students subsequently make use of procedural knowledge through practice. In this way, language acquisition can be viewed as a skill like any other. Declarative knowledge involves acquisition of isolated facts and rules (*e.g. knowing that a car can be driven*). Procedural knowledge requires practice and involve processing of longer units and increasing automization *(e.g. knowing how to drive a car)*. To gain a greater perspective, read DeKeyser (2015, Chapter 6).

declarative and procedural model According to this model, lexicon and grammar depend on two brain memory systems. Lexical memory depends on declarative memory, which supports the learning and use of fact- and event-based knowledge. Aspects of grammar, on the other hand, involve procedural memory. For more information, read Ullman (2015, Chapter 8).

developing system The developing system is a complex unit which evolves over time. It is normally represented as a network of forms and lexical items linked to each other via semantic, formal relationships and lexical relationships. Learners create a system based on these relationships, syntax and other competences (e.g., pragmatic, sociolinguistics). See VanPatten (2003, Chapter 3).

developmental sequences Learners seem to acquire particular structures (e.g. negation, question formation, etc.) in English, German, French, Italian and Japanese in a fixed and predictable order. For a broader discussion of this issue, read Pienemann and Lenzing (2015, Chapter 8).

discourse Samples of a language in context are known as 'discourse'. It comprises new and old information, but the flow of that information is presented in a coherent way. See Bardovi-Harlig (1994).

error analysis An approach to the study of second language acquisition and learners' errors that focuses on the internal processes of acquisition. 'The significance

of learners' errors', a paper by Corder (1967), provides new insights that allow us to better understand the sources of learners' errors.

explicit and implicit knowledge The role of explicit and implicit knowledge is still debated in SLA. SLA is implicit in nature, but adult learners engage in explicit learning. Implicit knowledge is associated with the notion of underlying competence and many scholars believe that it is the result of the interaction between universal grammar properties and input language. See Hulstijn (2005).

focus on form(s) There is a distinction to be drawn between 'focus on form' and 'focus on forms'. The latter refers to a type of instruction that isolates specific linguistic forms, and teaches them one at a time. The former is characterized by techniques which provide a focus on meaning and on form. See Spada (1997).

form–meaning connections Language-learners make good form–meaning connections when they are able to connect a form with its meaning in the input they receive (for example, when they understand that the morpheme *–ed* on the end of the verb in English refers to an event in the past). To gain a greater perspective, read VanPatten, Williams, Rott, and Overstreet (2004).

fossilization This refers to the cognitive processes/mechanisms that produce permanently stabilized interlanguage forms that remain in L2 learners' speech and/or writing over time without any difference to the input to which the learner is exposed and to what the learner does with that input. See Han (2013).

frequency This how often linguistic features appear in the input that learners hear or read. It is a key concept in the connectionist/emergentism theory. See Ellis (2002).

functionalism This approach sees language as a system of communication and links language knowledge to language use. It places an emphasis on the meaning of the elements of a sentence. To gain a greater perspective, read Bardovi-Harlig (2000, Chapter 4).

Fundamental Difference Hypothesis (FDH) The FDH states that the acquisition processes of children and adults differ fundamentally in terms of 'innate ability'. Children possess the innate ability to acquire the L1 grammar, whereas adults have lost it and, as a result, they approach the acquisition of a target language through problem-solving skills and attention. See Bley-Vromann (2009).

Fundamental Similarity Hypothesis (FSH) The FSH describes the process of L2 learning in adults. It sees all adult second language learning as fundamentally similar. To find out more about the FSH, read Robinson (1996, 1997).

heritage language This is a non-societal and non-majority language spoken by groups often known as linguistic minorities. See Valdés (2005).

incidental learning This refers to learners' ability to pick up aspects of language when their attention is actually on processing input. See Hulstijn (2001).

initial state The starting point for language learners, or what learners bring with themselves before they start acquiring a target (non-native) language. To gain a greater perspective, read White (2003).

input The language we hear or read and which has some kind of communicative intent. Learners use input to create a L2 grammar and it is a key ingredient in SLA. For more information, read VanPatten (2003, Chapter 2).

input enhancement A pedagogical intervention that concerns formal features of language and offers a kind of focus on form by highlighting features in various ways. See Sharwood Smith (1993).

input processing This is concerned with a number of fundamental questions related to the concept that acquisition involves the mapping of one form to one meaning. Input processing investigates the conditions under which learners make form–meaning connections in the input they attend to, why they sometimes fail to make these connections and the strategies they use to interpret the input. See VanPatten (2015, Chapter 7).

intake Learners process input as they attempt to understand the message it contains. They use input to make form–meaning connections and in so doing filter the input, which is then reduced and modified in a new entity called 'intake'. For more information, see Corder (1967).

Interaction Hypothesis The importance of interaction (both in terms of input modifications and feedback) is that it can bring something in the input to the learner's focal attention at a given moment, offering an opportunity to perceive and process some piece of language he or she might miss otherwise. See Gass and Mackey (2015, Chapter 10).

interlanguage This term refers to the intermediate state of learner language as it moves towards the target language. See Selinker (1972).

language acquisition device (LAD) Chomsky refers to humans' innate ability to learn languages as the language faculty. This was originally known as the language acquisition device (LAD) and later as Universal Grammar (UG). For more information, read White (2003, 2015).

learning strategies Students make use of a number of strategies to assist their own learning experience, including: metacognitive strategies; social strategies; cognitive strategies; and memory strategies. See O'Malley and Chamot (1990).

learning styles These refer to the ways in which learners perceive, process and develop input, information and language skills in a variety of ways. See Cohen (1998).

markedness This SLA concept refers to how typical or common a feature is. See Zobl (1981).

mental lexicon This refers to the arrangement of words in one's mind. It is like a 'mental dictionary' where words, and the information related to them (meaning, inflections, pronunciation, etc.), are stored. See Jackendoff (2002).

mental representation Competence, or mental representation, is the 'stuff' that learners have in their heads about language: the unconscious, implicit, and generally abstract knowledge of language. Skill in speaking (or writing) does not always demonstrate what is in our mental representation. To gain a greater perspective, read VanPatten and Rothman (2013).

metalinguistic knowledge This is conscious knowledge about the language itself, and is usually demonstrated through talking about the language. To gain a greater perspective you should read Roehr (2008)

Monitor Theory According to the Monitor Theory, L2 classrooms need to mimic the environment in which L1 learning takes place. Krashen hypothesized that if L2 learners were exposed to 'comprehensible' input and were provided with opportunities to focus on meaning and messages rather than grammatical forms and accuracy, they would be able to acquire the L2 in much the same way as they had their L1. See Krashen (1982).

motivation Motivation can be described and measured as learners' positive disposition towards the L2 and the desire to interact with the environment and become a valued member of the community. See Dorney (2001).

morpheme studies *see* **acquisition orders**

multilingualism The learning of more than two languages has been referred to as 'multilingualism'. See Hufeisen (1998).

negative evidence There are two types of negative evidence: direct and indirect. Direct negative evidence refers to feedback in which the learner is explicitly told his or her utterance is incorrect in some way. Indirect negative evidence refers to conversational interactions in which the person speaking with the learner implicitly points out something is wrong (negotiation

of meaning). For more information, read Nassaji (2015).

negotiation of meaning This is the process in which learners attempt to understand a certain meaning through participating in the conversation actively and attempting to figure out the meaning. To gain a greater perspective, read Lyster and Ranta (1997).

neurolinguistics This is the science that investigates the role of brain function in comprehending, producing, and storing language data. See Paradis (2004).

noticing Bringing a form to someone's attention is no guarantee that it will get processed. Noticing means that learners are becoming aware of something in the input and that there is some level of awareness in learning. See Schmidt (2001).

output This refers to a language that learners produce and which has a communicative purpose. Learners make output by drawing on their network of connections (developing system). Learners must activate lexical items and grammatical forms to express particular meaning. They make use of production strategies to retrieve and exchange grammatical information. See VanPatten (2003, Chapter 4).

overgeneralization This is a process that occurs as a second language is learned and where learners generalize learned rules for items which are not subject to those rules. See Larsen-Freeman and Long (1991).

parameters Parameters are particular variations of a type of syntactic feature. To gain a greater perspective, see White (2015).

performance This refers to the use of language to communicate. This term contrasts directly with competence. To gain a greater perspective, read Chomsky (1965).

parsing Parsing is how learners compute syntactic relationships in real time while listening or reading. L2 learners must be able to determine, for example, which is the subject and which the object in a sentence they hear or read. See Frenck-Mestre (2005).

positive evidence Positive evidence can be described as input modifications which can bring something in the input into the learner's focal attention, offering an opportunity to perceive and process some piece of language he or she might miss otherwise. See Wong (2005).

poverty of the stimulus This refers to the fact that learners happen to know more than they are expected or supposed to know based on the data they have been exposed to. For more information, read Bley-Vroman (1990)

pragmatics Pragmatics is a branch of linguistics dealing with the investigation of language in context and how humans use language (sentences) to express meaning. See Bardovi-Harlig and Vellenga (2012).

Processability Theory This states that learners acquire morphological and syntactic forms in a predictable sequence. This sequence is consistent across learners. To gain a greater perspective, read Pienemann (1998).

processing strategies These are the methods that learners employ when mapping form onto meaning. See VanPatten and Benati (2010).

processing instruction This is a pedagogical intervention that is psycholinguistically motivated (i.e. it has an explicit focus on form) and which gives learners explicit information concerning the target item, and activities containing structured input. See VanPatten and Benati (2010).

restructuring This refers to internal changes in language development. Language data is processed and accommodated in the new system and this might have a number of effects on the development of grammar. The U-shaped learning curve is a typical example of restructuring. See McLaughlin (1990).

Socio-cultural Theory The main concept in the theory is that human mental function is generated by participating in the cultural mediation integrated into social activities. See Lantolf, Thorne and Poehner (2015, Chapter 11).

scaffolding Scaffolding refers to any kind of adult–child or expert–novice assisted performance. Its focus does not lie in mediation, quality or even type of assistance. See Donato (1994).

sensitive period The milder version of a critical period for language acquisition is the sensitive period. It refers to varying ends of the offset for sub-parts of language. The cut-off point is unclear and loss of language-learning abilities is gradual. See Oyama (1976).

Skill Acquisition Theory According to this model, learners move from declarative to procedural knowledge. Speed and accuracy improve as the learners become more automatic in their performance. This view opposes the idea that knowledge gained through language 'learning' cannot turn into 'acquisition'. See Anderson (1983).

Shallow Structure Hypothesis (SSH) This argues that during real-time language comprehension, L2 learners can only construct shallow structure representations, relying almost exclusively on lexical and semantic information. See Clahsen and Felser (2006).

sociolinguistics The study of how language functions in society and of the interaction between linguistic and social variables. Sociolinguistics also focuses on how language is realized in social and cultural contexts and its changes among groups and communities over time. See Holmes (2001).

subjacency This refers to the concept of syntactic movement. Phrases are said to travel from one position to another position in a sentence. There are a growing number of studies measuring this phenomenon; for more information, see Cook and Newson (2007).

Teachability Hypothesis According to the Teachability Hypothesis, not everything that is taught can necessarily be also learned. In other words, the effects of instructed language learning on the development of the interlanguage system depend on the developmental stage of the learner. See Pienemann and Lenzing (2015).

transfer Transfer is a concept that has been defined from various perspectives. It is dependent on learners' exposure to input from the environment, as well as to use and internal self-organization. Transfer is seen as a constraint, implying that within the target language's development, learners make non-target-like productions because they make hypotheses which are constrained by the influence of their L1. See Odlin (2003).

ultimate attainment Sometimes referred to as 'end state', this term refers to the degree to which L2 learners can develop native-like competence across different language domains. See White and Genesee (1996).

Universal Grammar Theory According to the Universal Grammar Theory, learning the grammar of a second language is simply a matter of setting the correct parameters. Universal Grammar also provides a succinct explanation for much of the phenomenon of language transfer. See White (2015, Chapter 3).

uptake Uptake refers to the immediate response from L2 learners to the corrective feedback received about their utterances. See Lyster and Ranta (1997).

variability Sometimes referred to as 'variation', this refers to situations in which we encounter differential ultimate attainments within an individual learner's system – specifically, where particular sub-systems successfully reach the end-state and others do not. To gain a greater perspective, read Gass *et al.* (2013)

working memory This is the memory in humans that receives input and is responsible for transferring this input to long-term memory, which is capable of storing information for a longer period. See Baddeley and Hitch (1994).

zone of proximal development (ZPD) This refers to the level of performance of which a learner is capable when there is support from negotiation with an expert or adult. See Vygotsky (1978).

References

Anderson, J. (1983). *The Architecture of Cognition*. Cambridge, MA: Harvard University Press.

Andersen, R. W. (1984). The one-to-one principle of interlanguage construction. *Language Learning, 34*, 77–95.

Andersen, R. W. (1990). Model, processes, principles and strategies: Second language acquisition inside and outside the classroom. In B. VanPatten and J. F. Lee (eds), *Second Language Acquisition: Foreign Language Learning* (pp. 45–78). Clevedon: Multilingual Matters.

Andersen, R. W., and Shirai, Y. (1994). Discourse motivations for some cognitive acquisition principles. *Studies in Second Language Acquisition, 16*, 133–56.

Angelovska, T., and Hahn, A. (2014). Raising language awareness for learning and teaching L3 grammar. In A. Benati, C. Laval and M. Arche (eds), *The Grammar Dimension in Instructed Second Language Learning* (pp. 185–207). London: Bloomsbury Academic.

Archibald, J. (2005). Second language acquisition. In W. O'Grady, J. Archibald, M. Aronoff and J. Reseller (eds), *Contemporary Linguistics: An Introduction* (pp. 2–15). New York: Bedford.

Atkinson, D. (ed.). (2011). *Alternative Approaches in Second Language Acquisition*. New York: Routledge.

Bachman, L. F. (1990). *Fundamental Considerations in Language Testing*. Oxford: Oxford University Press.

Bachman, L. F., and Palmer, A. S. (1996). *Language Testing in Practice: Designing and Developing Useful Language Tests*. Oxford: Oxford University Press.

Baddeley, A. (2003). Working memory and language: An overview. *Journal of Communication Disorders, 36*, 189–208.

Baddeley A. D., and Hitch G. J. (1994) Developments in the concept of working memory. *Neuropsychology, 8*, 485–493.

Bardovi-Harlig, K. (1994). Anecdote or evidence? Evaluating support for hypotheses concerning the development of tense and aspect. In E. Tarone, S. Gass and A. Cohen (eds), *Research Methodology in Second Language Acquisition*. Hillsdale, NJ: Lawrence Erlbaum Associates.

Bardovi-Harlig, K. (1998). Narrative structure and lexical aspect: Conspiring factors in second language acquisition of tense-aspect morphology. *Studies in Second Language Acquisition, 20*, 471–508.

Bardovi-Harlig, K. (2000). *Tense and Aspect in Second Language Acquisition: Form, Meaning and Use*. Oxford, England: Blackwell.

Bardovi-Harlig, K. (2015). One functional approach to SLA. In B. VanPatten and J. Williams (eds), *Theories in Second Language Acquisition* (2nd ed.; pp. 54–74). New York: Routledge.

Bardovi-Harlig, K., and Vellenga, H. E. (2012). The effect of instruction on conventional expressions in L2 pragmatics. *System*, 40, 77–89.

Beebe, L. M., and Giles, H. (1984). Speech-accommodation theories: A discussion in terms of second language acquisition. *International Journal of the Sociology of Language*, 46, 5–32.

Benati, A. (2013). *Issues in Second Language Teaching*. Sheffield: Equinox.

Benati, A. (2015). *Second Language Research: Key Methodological Frameworks*. Sheffield: Equinox Publishing.

Benati, A., and Lee, J. (2008). *Grammar Acquisition and Processing Instruction*. Clevedon: Multilingual Matters.

Bhatia, T. K., and Ritchie, W. C. (2004). *The Handbook of Bilingualism*. Oxford: Blackwell.

Bialystok, E. (1997). The structure of age: In search of barriers to second language acquisition. *Second Language Research*, 13, 116–137.

Bialystok, E., and Hakuta, K. (1994). *In Other Words: The Science and Psychology of Second-Language Acquisition*. New York: Basic Books.

Birdsong, D. (1992). Ultimate attainment in second language acquisition. *Language*, 68, 706–755.

Birdsong, D. (2005). Interpreting age effects in second language acquisition. In J. F. Kroll and A. M. B. de Groot (eds), *Handbook of Bilingualism: Psycholinguistic Approaches* (pp. 109–127). Oxford: Oxford University Press.

Birdsong, D. (2006). Age and second language acquisition and processing: A selective overview. *Language Learning*, 56, 9–49.

Birdsong, D., and Molis, M. (2001). On the evidence for maturational constraints in second language acquisition. *Journal of Memory and Language*, 44, 235–249.

Birdsong, D., and Paik, J. (2008). Second language acquisition and ultimate attainment. In B. Spolsky and F. Hult (eds), *Handbook of Educational Linguistics* (pp. 424–436). Oxford: Blackwell Publishing.

Bley-Vroman, R. (1990). The logical problem of foreign language learning. *Linguistic Analysis*, 20, 3–49.

Bley-Vroman, R. (2009). The evolving context of the Fundamental Difference Hypothesis. *Studies in Second Language Acquisition*, 31, 175–198.

Bongaerts, T., van Summeren, C., Planken, B. and Schils, E. (1997). Age and ultimate attainment in the pronunciation of a foreign language. *Studies in Second Language Acquisition*, 19, 447–465.

Brantmeier, C. (ed.) (2009). *Crossing Languages and Research Methods: Analyses of Adult Foreign Language Reading*. Greenwich, CT: Information Age Publishing.

Canale, M. (1983). From communicative competence to communicative language pedagogy. In J. C. Richards and R. W. Schmidt (eds), *Language and Communication* (pp. 2–27). Harlow: Longman.

Canale, M. (1984). A communicative approach to language proficiency assessment in a minority setting. In C. Rivera (ed.), *Communicative Competence Approaches to Language Proficiency Assessment: Research and Application* (pp. 107–122). Clevedon: Multilingual Matters.

Canale, M., and Swain, M. (1980). Theoretical bases of communicative approaches to second language teaching and testing. *Applied Linguistics*, 1, 1–47.

Carroll, J. (1981). Twenty-five years of research on foreign language aptitude. In
  K. C. Diller (ed.), *Individual Differences and Universals in Language Learning
  Aptitude* (pp. 83–117). Rowley, MA: Newbury House.

Celce-Murcia M., Dörnyei, Z., and Thurrell, S. (1995). Communicative competence:
  A pedagogically motivated model with content specifications. *Issues in Applied
  Linguistics*, 6, 5–35.

Cenoz, J., and Gorter, D. (2011). A holistic approach to multilingual education:
  Introduction. *The Modern Language Journal*, 95, 339–343.

Chomsky, N. (1959). A review of B. F. Skinner's *Verbal Behavior*. *Language*,
  35, 26–58.

Chomsky, N. (1965). *Aspects of the Theory of Syntax*. Cambridge, MA: MIT
  Press.

Chomsky, N. (1981). *Lectures on Government and Binding*. Dordrecht: Foris.

Clahsen, H. (1988). Parameterized grammatical theory and language acquisition: A
  study of the acquisition of verb placement and inflection by children and adults.
  In S. Flynn and W. O'Neil. (eds), (1988). *Linguistic Theory in Second Language
  Acquisition* (pp. 47–75). Dordrecht: Kluwer.

Clahsen, H., and C. Felser (2006). How native-like is non-native language
  processing? *Trends in Cognitive Sciences*, 10, 564–570.

Clahsen, H., and Muysken, P. (1986). The availability of universal grammar to adult
  and child learners: A study of the acquisition of German word order. *Second
  Language Research*, 2, 93–119.

Clahsen, H., and Muysken, P. (1989). The UG paradox in L2 acquisition, *Language
  Research* 5, 1–29.

Cohen, A. D. (1998). *Strategies in Learning and Using a Second Language*. Harlow:
  Longman.

Conway, A. R. A., Jarrold, C., Kane, M. J., Miyake, A., and Towse, J. N. (eds),
  (2007). *Variation in Working Memory*. New York: Oxford University Press.

Cook, V. J. (ed.) (2003). *Effects of the Second Language on the First*. Clevedon:
  Multilingual Matters.

Cook, V. J., and Newson, M. (2007). *Chomsky's Universal Grammar: An
  Introduction*. Oxford: Blackwell Publishing.

Coppieters, R. (1987). Competence differences between native and near-native
  speakers. *Language*, 63, 544–573.

Corder, S. Pit. (1967). The significance of learners' errors. *International Review of
  Applied Linguistics* 5, 161–170.

Corder, S. Pit (1981). *Error Analysis and Interlanguage*. Oxford: Oxford University
  Press.

Curtiss, S. (1977). *Genie: A Psycholinguistic Study of a Modern Day 'Wild Child'*.
  New York, NY: Academic Press.

De Angelis G. (2007). *Third or Additional Language Acquisition*. Clevedon:
  Multilingual Matters.

de Bot, K. (1992). A bilingual processing model: Levelt's 'speaking' model adapted.
  Applied Linguistics, 13, 1–24.

de Bot, K., and Jaensch, C. (2015). What is special about L3 processing?
  Bilingualism: Language and Cognition, 18, 130–144.

De Houwer, A. (1995). Bilingual language acquisition. In P. Fletcher and
  B. MacWhinney, *A Handbook of Child Language* (pp. 219–250). Oxford:
  Blackwell.

DeKeyser, R. (2000). The robustness of critical period effects in second language learners. *Studies in Second Language Acquisition*, 22, 499–533.

DeKeyser, R. (2007). Skill Acquisition Theory. In B. VanPatten and J. Williams (eds), *Theories in Second Language Acquisition: An Introduction* (pp. 97–112). Mahwah, NJ: Lawrence Erlbaum Associates.

DeKeyser, R. (2015). Skill Acquisition Theory. In B. VanPatten and J. Williams (eds), *Theories in Second Language Acquisition* (2nd ed.; pp. 94–112). New York: Routledge.

DeKeyser, R. M., and Larson-Hall, J. (2005). What does the critical period really mean? In J. F. Kroll and A. M. B. de Groot (eds), *Handbook of Bilingualism: Psycholinguistic Approaches* (pp. 89–108). Oxford: Oxford University Press.

Deuchar, M., and S. Quay. (2000). *Bilingual Acquisition: Theoretical Implications of a Case Study*. New York: Oxford University Press.

Donato, R. (1994). Collective scaffolding in second language learning. In J. P. Lantolf and G. Appel (eds), *Vygotskian Approaches to Second Language Research* (pp. 33–56). Westport, CT: Ablex Publishing

Dörnyei, Z. (2001). *Teaching and Researching Motivation*. Harlow: Longman.

Dörnyei, Z. (2006). Individual differences in second language acquisition. In K. Bardovi-Harlig and Z. Dörnyei (eds), *Themes in SLA research AILA Review* (pp. 42–68). Amsterdam: John Benjamins Publishing.

Dörnyei Z., and Skehan P. (2003). Individual differences in second language learning. In C. Doughty and M. Long (eds), *Handbook of Second Language Acquisition* (pp. 589–630). Oxford: Blackwell.

Dörnyei, Z., and Ushioda, E. (2011). *Teaching and Researching Motivation*. Harlow: Longman.

Doughty, C. J. (2003). Instructed SLA: Constraints, compensation, and enhancement. In C. Doughty and M. Long (eds), *The Handbook of Second Language Acquisition* (pp. 256–310). Oxford: Blackwell.

Doughty, C. J., and Long, M. (eds), (2003). *The Handbook of Second Language Acquisition*. Oxford: Blackwell.

du Plessis, J., Solin, D., Travis, L., and White, L. (1987). UG or not UG, that is the question: a reply to Clahsen and Muysken. *Second Language Research*, 3, 56–75.

Ellis, N. C. (2002). Reflections on frequency effects in language processing. *Studies in Second Language Acquisition*, 24, 297–339.

Ellis, N. C. (2005). At the interface: Dynamic interactions of explicit and implicit language knowledge. *Studies in Second Language Acquisition*, 27, 305–352.

Ellis, N. C. (2012). Frequency-based accounts of SLA. In S. M. Gass and A. Mackey (eds), *Handbook of Second Language Acquisition* (pp. 193–210). London: Routledge.

Ellis, N., and Wulff, S. (2015). Usage-based approaches to SLA. In B. VanPatten and J. Williams (eds), *Theories in Second Language Acquisition* (pp. 75–93). New York: Routledge.

Ellis, R. (2008). *SLA Research and Language Teaching*. New York: Oxford University Press.

Ellis, R., and Shintani, N. (2013). *Exploring Language Pedagogy through Second Language Acquisition Research*. London: Routledge.

Elsner, D., and Keßler, J.-U. (ed.) (2013). *Bilingual Education in Primary School: Aspects of Immersion, CLIL, and Bilingual Modules*. Tübingen: Narr

Epstein, S. D., Flynn, S., and Martohardjono, G. (1996) Second language acquisition: Theoretical and experimental issues in contemporary research. *Behavioral and Brain Sciences*, 19, 677–758.

Eskildsen, S. W. (2009). Constructing another language: usage-based linguistics in second language acquisition. *Applied Linguistics*, 30, 335–357.

Field, J. (2008). *Listening in the Language Classroom*. Cambridge: Cambridge University Press.

Flege, J. E. (1999). Age of learning and second language speech. In D. Birdsong (ed.), *Second Language Acquisition and the Critical Period Hypothesis* (pp. 101–131). Mahwah, NJ: Lawrence Erlbaum Associates.

Flynn, S. (1996). A parameter-setting approach to second language acquisition. In W. Ritchie and T. Bhatia (eds), *Handbook of Language Acquisition* (pp. 121–158). San Diego: Academic Press.

Flynn, S., and Martohardjono, G. (1994). Mapping from the initial state to the final state: The separation of universal principles and language-specific principles. In B. Lust, M. Suner and J. Whitman (eds), *Syntactic Theory and First Language Acquisition: Crosslinguistic Perspectives. Vol. 1: Heads, Projections and Learnability* (pp. 319–335). Hillsdale, NJ: Lawrence Erlbaum Associates.

Frenck-Mestre, C. (2005). Eye-movement recording as a tool for studying syntactic processing in a second language. *Second Language Research, 21*, 175–198.

Gardner, R. (2001). Language learning motivation: The student, the teacher, and the researcher. *Texas Papers in Foreign Language Education*, 6, 1–18.

Gass, S. (1997). *Input, Interaction, and the Second Language Learner*. Mahwah, NJ: Lawrence Erlbaum Associates.

Gass, S., and Mackey, A. (2015). Input, interaction and output in second language acquisition. In B. VanPatten and J. Williams (eds), *Theories in Second Language Acquisition* (pp. 180–206). New York: Routledge.

Gass, S. M., and Selinker, L. (2008). *Second Language Acquisition: An Introductory Course*. New York: Routledge.

Gass, S., Behney, J. and Plonsky, L. (2013). *Second Language Acquisition: An Introductory Course (4th ed.)* NewYork: Taylor and Francis

Giles, H., and Smith, P. (1979). Accommodation Theory: Optimal levels of convergence. In H. Giles and R. St. Clair (eds), *Language and Social Psychology* (pp. 45–65). Oxford: Basil Blackwell.

Givón, T. (1979). From discourse to syntax: Grammar as a processing strategy. In T. Givón (ed.), *Syntax and semantics. Discourse and syntax* (Vol.12). New York: Academic Press.

Green, D. W. (1986). Control, activation and resource. *Brain and Language*, 27, 210–223. a

Greenberg, J. H. (1991). Typology/universals and second language acquisition. In T. Huebner and A. Ferguson (eds), *Second Language Acquisition and Linguistic Theories* (pp. 37–43). Amsterdam: John Benjamins Publishing.

Grenfell, M., and Macaro, E. (2007). Claims and critiques. In A. D. Cohen and E. Macaro (eds), *Language Learner Strategies: 30 Years of Research and Practice* (pp. 9–28). Oxford: Oxford University Press.

Grosjean, F. (1982). *Life with Two Languages: An Introduction to Bilingualism*. Cambridge, MA: Harvard University Press

Grosjean, F. (1992). Another view of bilingualism. In Harris, R. (ed.). *Cognitive Processing in Bilinguals* (pp. 51–62). Amsterdam: North-Holland.

Guilloteaux, M. J., and Dörnyei, Z. (2008). Motivating language learners: A classroom-oriented investigation of the effects of motivational strategies on student motivation. *TESOL Quarterly*, 42, 55–77.

Han, Z. H. (2013). Forty years later: Updating the Fossilization Hypothesis. *Language Teaching*, 46, 133–71.

Hawkins, R., and Yuet-hung Chan, C. (1997). The partial availability of Universal Grammar in second language acquisition: The 'failed functional features hypothesis'. *Second Language Research*, 13, 187–226.

Holmes, J. (2001). *An Introduction to Sociolinguistics*. Harlow: Pearson Education Limited.

Hufeisen, B. (1998). L3 – Stand der Forschung – Was bleibt zu tun? In B. Hufeisen and B. Lindemann (eds), *Tertiärsprachen. Theorien, Modelle, Methoden* (pp. 169–183). Tübingen: Stauffenburg.

Hulstijn, J. (2001). Intentional and incidental second language vocabulary learning: A reappraisal of elaboration, rehearsal and automaticity. In P. Robinson (ed.), *Cognition and Second Language Instruction* (pp. 258–287). Cambridge: Cambridge University Press.

Hulstijn, J. (2005). Theoretical and empirical issues in the study of implicit and explicit second language learning: introduction. *Studies in Second Language Acquisition*, 27, 129–140.

Hymes, D. H. (1972). On communicative competence. In J. B. Pride and J. Holmes (eds), *Sociolinguistics* (pp. 269–293). London: Penguin.

Jackendoff, R. S. (2002). *Foundations of Language: Brain, Meaning, Grammar, and Evolution*. Oxford: Oxford University Press.

Jenkins, J. (2015). *Global Englishes: A Resource Book for Students*. Abingdon: Routledge.

Jessner, U. (2013). Teaching a third language. In C. A. Chapelle (ed.), *The Encyclopedia of Applied Linguistics* (pp. 5662–5665). New York: Wiley-Blackwell.

Johnson, J. S., and Newport, E. (1989). Critical period effects in second language learning: The influence of maturational state on the acquisition of English as a second language. *Cognitive Psychology*, 21, 60–99.

Johnson, J. S., and Newport, E. (1991). Critical period effects on universal properties of language: The status of subjacency in the acquisition of a second language. *Cognition*, 39, 215–58.

Johnstone, R. (2002). *Addressing the Age Factor: Some Implications for Languages Policy*. Stransbourg: Coucil of Europe. (URL: http://www.coe.int/t/dg4/linguistic/Source/JohnstoneEN.pdf)

Kim K. H., Relkin N. R., Lee K. M., and Hirsch J. (1997). Distinct cortical areas associated with native and second languages. *Nature*, 388, 171–4.

Klein, W. (2009). Concepts of time. In W. Klein and P. Li (eds), *The Expression of Time* (pp. 5–38). Berlin: Mouton de Gruyter.

Klein, W., and Dimroth, C. (2009). Untutored second language acquisition. In W. C. Ritchie and T. K. Bhatia (eds), *The New Handbook of Second Language Acquisition* (pp. 503–522). Bingley: Emerald.

Kowal, M., and Swain, M. (1997). From semantic to syntactic processing. In R. Johnson and M. Swain (eds), *Immersion Education: International Perspectives* (pp. 284–309). Cambridge: Cambridge University Press.

Krashen, S. (1981). *Second Language Acquisition and Second Language Learning*. Oxford: Pergamon.

Krashen, S. (1985). *The Input Hypothesis: Issues and Implications*. Oxford: Pergamon Press.

Krashen, S. (2009). The comprehension hypothesis extended. In T. Piske and M. Young-Scholten (eds), *Input Matters* (pp. 81–94). Bristol: Multilingual Matters.

Kuhl, P. K. (2010). Brain mechanisms in early language acquisition. *Neuron* 67, 713–727.

Lado, R. (1957). *Linguistics Across Cultures: Applied Linguistics for Language Teachers*. Ann Arbor, MI: University of Michigan Press.

Lantolf, J., Thorne, S., and Poehner, E. (2015). Sociocultural theory and second language development. In B. VanPatten and J. Williams (eds), *Theories in Second Language Acquisition* (2nd ed.; pp. 207–226). New York: Routledge.

Larsen-Freeman, D. (1976). An explanation for the morpheme acquisition order of second language learners. *Language Learning*, 26, 125–134.

Larsen-Freeman, D. (2002). Language acquisition and language use from a chaos/complexity theory perspective. In C. Kramsch (ed.), *Language Acquisition and Language Socialization: Ecological Perspectives* (pp. 33–46). London: Continuum.

Larsen-Freeman, D. (2015). Complexity Theory. In B. VanPatten and J. Williams (eds), *Theories in Second Language Acquisition* (pp. 227–244). New York: Routledge.

Larsen-Freeman, D., and Long, M. H. (1991). *An Introduction to Second Language Acquisition Research*. New York: Longman.

Lee, J. and VanPatten, B. (2003). *Making Communicative Classrooms Happen*. New York: McGraw-Hill.

Lenneberg, E. H. (1967). *Biological Foundations of Language*. New York: Wiley.

Leow, R. P. (1997). Attention, awareness, and foreign language behavior. *Language Learning*, 47, 467–506. In C. Doughty and J. Williams (eds), *Focus on Form in Classroom Second Language Acquisition*. Cambridge: Cambridge University Press.

Lightbown, P., and Spada, N. (2001). Recasts as feedback to language learners. *Language Learning*, 52, 719–758.

Lightbown, P., and Spada, N. (2008). *How Languages Are Learned* (3rd ed.). Oxford: Oxford University Press.

Lightbown, P. M. & Spada, N. (2013). *How Languages Are Learned* (4th ed.). Oxford: Oxford University Press

Lyster, R., and Ranta, L. (1997). Corrective feedback and learner uptake: Negotiation of form in communicative classrooms. *Studies in Second Language Acquisition*, 19, 37–66.

Long, M. (1996). The role of the linguistic environment in second language acquisition. In W. Ritchie and T. Bhatia (eds), *Handbook of Second Language Acquisition* (pp. 413–68). San Diego: Academic Press.

Long, M. (2007). *Problems in SLA*. Mahwah, NJ: Lawrence Erlbaum Associates.

MacWhinney B. (1987). The competition model. In B. MacWhinney (ed.), *Mechanism of Language Acquisition* (pp. 249–308). Hillsdale, NJ: Lawrence Erlbaum Associates.

MacWhinney, B. (2001). The Competition Model: The input, the context, and the brain. In P. Robinson (ed.), *Cognition and Second Language Instruction* (pp. 249–308). New York: Cambridge University Press.

Marinova-Todd, S. H., Marshall, D. B., and Snow, C. E. (2000). Three misconceptions about age and second language acquisition. *TESOL Quarterly*, 34, 9–34.

Martin, K., and Ellis, N. (2012). The roles of phonological short-term memory and working memory in L2 grammar and vocabulary learning. *Studies in Second Language Acquisition*, 34, 349–379.

McLaughlin, B (1990). Restructuring. *Applied Linguistics*, 11, 113–128.

McLaughlin, B (1987). *Theories of Second Language Learning*. London: Edward Arnold.

Meisel, J. (2011). *First and Second Language Acquisition*. Cambridge: Cambridge University Press.

Muñoz, C. (ed.) (2006). *Age and the Rate of Foreign Language Learning*. Clevedon: Multilingual Matters.

Nassaji, H. (2011). Correcting students' written grammatical errors: The effects of negotiated versus non-negotiated feedback. *Studies in Second Language Learning and Teaching*, 1, 315–334.

Nassaji, H. (2015). *The Interactional Feedback Dimension on Instructed Second Language Learning*. London: Bloomsbury.

Nassaji, H., and Fotos, S. (2011). *Teaching Grammar in Second Language Classrooms*. New York: Routledge.

Nassaji, H., and Swain, M. (2000). A Vygotskian perspective on corrective feedback: The effect of random versus negotiated help on the learning of English articles. *Language Awareness*, 9, 34–51.

Newport, E. (1990). Maturational constraints on language learning. *Cognitive Science*, 14, 11–28

Nikolov, M. (2000). The Critical Period Hypothesis reconsidered: Successful adult learners of Hungarian and English. *IRAL (International Review of Applied Linguistics in Language Teaching)*. Volume 38, Issue 2, 109–12.

Nunan, D. (1994). Linguistic theory and pedagogic practice. In T. Odlin (ed.), *Perspectives on Pedagogical Grammar*. Cambridge: Cambridge University Press.

Nunan, D. (2004). *Task-based Language Teaching*. Cambridge: Cambridge University Press

Odlin, T. (1989). *Language Transfer*. Cambridge: Cambridge University Press.

Odlin, T. (2003) Cross-linguistic influence. In C. Doughty and M. Long (eds), *Handbook of Second Language Acquisition* (pp. 436–486). Oxford: Blackwell.

O'Malley, J. M., and Chamot, A. U. (1990). *Learning Strategies in Second Language Acquisition*. Cambridge: Cambridge University Press.

Ortega, L. (ed.). (2015). *Second Language Acquisition* (2nd ed.). London: Routledge.

Ortega, L., Cumming, A., Ellis, N. C. (eds), (2013). *Agendas for Language Learning Research*. Malden, MA: Wiley-Blackwell.

Oxford, R. L. (1990). *Language Learning Strategies: What Every Teacher Should Know*. Boston: Heinle and Heinle.

Oxford, R. L. (1999). Learning strategies. In B. Spolsky (ed.), *Concise Encyclopedia of Educational Linguistics* (pp. 518–522). Oxford, UK: Elsevier.

Oyama, S. (1976). A sensitive period for the acquisition of a nonnative phonological system. *Journal of Psycholinguistic Research*, 5, 261–283.

Paradis, M. (2004). *A Neurolinguistic Theory of Bilingualism*. Amsterdam: John Benjamins Publishing.

Penfield, W. and Roberts, L. (1959). *Speech and Brain Mechanisms*. Princeton, NJ: Princeton University Press.

Perani, D., Dehaene, S., Grassi, F., Cohen, L., Cappa, S. F., Dupoux, E., Fazio F. and Mehler, J. (1996). Brain processing of native and foreign languages. *Neuroreport*, 7, 2439–2444.

Perani, D., Paulesu, E., Sebastian-Galles, N., Dupoux, E., Dehaene, S., Bettinardi, V., *et al.* (1998) The bilingual brain: proficiency and age of acquisition of the second language. *Brain* 121, 1841–52

Pienemann, M. (1998) *Language Processing and Second Language development: Processability Theory.* Amsterdam: John Benjamins Publishing.

Pienemann, M. (2007). Processability Theory. In B. VanPatten and J. Williams (eds), *Theories in Second Language Acquisition: An introduction.* New York: Routledge.

Pienemann, M., and Lenzing, A. (2015). Processability theory. In B. VanPatten and J. Williams (eds), *Theories in Second Language Acquisition* (2nd ed.; pp. 159–179). New York: Routledge.

Piske, T. (2013) Bilingual education: Chances and challenges. In D. Elsner and J. U. Keßler (eds), *Bilingual Education in Primary School: Aspects of Immersion, CLIL, and Bilingual Modules* (pp. 28–40). Tübingen: Narr.

Richards, J. C., and Schmidt, R. (eds), (2010). *Longman Dictionary of Language Teaching and Applied Linguistics.* Harlow: Pearson Education Ltd.

Robinson, P. (1996). Learning simple and complex second language rules under implicit, incidental, rule-search, and instructed conditions. *Studies in Second Language Acquisition*, 18, 27–67.

Robinson, P. (1997). Individual differences and the fundamental similarity of implicit and explicit adult second language learning. *Language Learning*, 47, 45–99.

Robinson, P. (2001). Individual differences, cognitive abilities, aptitude complexes and learning conditions in second language acquisition. *Second Language Research*, 17, 368–92.

Robinson, P. (2003). Attention and memory during SLA. In C. Doughty and M. Long, (eds), *The Handbook of Second Language Acquisition* (pp. 631–679). Oxford: Blackwell.

Robinson, P. (ed.) (2012). *Routledge Encyclopedia of Second Language Acquisition.* New York: Routledge.

Roehr, K. (2008). Metalinguistic knowledge and language ability in university-level L2 learners. *Applied Linguistics*, 29, 173–199.

Ryan, R., and Deci, E. (2000). Intrinsic and extrinsic motivations: classic definitions and new directions. *Contemporary Educational Psychology*, 25, 54–67.

Savignon, S (2005). *Communicative Competence: Theory and Classroom Practice.* New York: McGraw-Hill.

Schachter, J. (1974). An error in error analysis. *Language Learning*, *24*, 205–214.

Schmidt, R. (1990). The role of consciousness in language learning. *Applied Linguistics* 11, 17–46, 129–158.

Schmidt, R. (1995). *Attention and Awareness in Foreign Language Learning.* Manoa: University of Hawai'i.

Schmidt, R. (2001). Attention. In P. Robinson (ed.), *Cognition and Second Language Instruction* (pp. 3–32). Cambridge: Cambridge University Press.

Schumann, J. H. (1978). *The Pidgination Process: A Model for Second Language Acquisition.* Rowley, MA: Newbury House.

Schumm, J. S. (ed.) (2006). *Reading Assessment and Instruction for All Learners.* New York: Guilford Press.

Schwartz, B., and Sprouse, R. (1996). L2 cognitive states and the full transfer/full access model. *Second Language Research*, 12, 40–72.

Schwartz, B., and Tomaselli, A. (1990). Some implications from an analysis of German word order. In A. Werner, W. Kosmeijer and E. Reuland (eds), *Issues in Germanic Syntax* (pp. 251–274). Berlin: Walter de Gruyter.

Schwieter, J. W. (2010). *Cognition and Bilingual Speech: Psycholinguistic Aspects of Language Production, Processing, and Inhibitory Control.* Saarbrücken: Lambert Academic.

Schwieter, J. W. (ed.) (2013). *Innovative Research and Practices in Second Language Acquisition and Bilingualism.* Amsterdam/Philadelphia, PA: John Benjamins Publishing.

Schwieter, J. W. (ed.) (2015). *The Cambridge Handbook of Bilingual Processing.* Cambridge: Cambridge University Press.

Seidlhofer, B. (2011). *Understanding English as a* Lingua Franca. Oxford: Oxford University Press.

Selinker, L. (1972). Interlanguage. *International Review of Applied Linguistics*, 10, 209–231.

Selinker, L., and Lamendella, J. (1978). Two perspectives on fossilization in interlanguage learning. *Interlanguage Studies Bulletin*, 3, 143–91.

Sharwood Smith, M. (1993). Input enhancement in instructed SLA: Theoretical bases. *Studies in Second Language Acquisition*, 15, 165–179.

Sharwood Smith, M., and Kellerman, E. (1986). Crosslinguistic influence in second language: an introduction. In E. Kellerman and M. Sharwood Smith (eds), *Crosslinguistic Influence in Second Language Acquisition* (pp. 1–9). Oxford: Pergamon.

Sheen, Y. (2011). *Corrective Feedback, Individual Differences and Second Language Learning.* New York: Springer.

Şimşek, S. C. (2006). *Third Language Acquisition: Turkish-German Bilingual Students' Acquisition of English Word Order in a German Educational Setting.* Münster: Waxmann.

Singleton, D. (2001). Age and second language acquisition. *Annual Review of Applied Linguistics*, 21, 77–89.

Singleton, D. (2007). The critical period hypothesis: Some problems. *Interlinguistica*, 17, 48–56.

Skehan, P. (1998). *A Cognitive Approach to Learning Language.* Oxford: Oxford University Press.

Skinner, B. F. (1957). *Verbal Behavior.* New York: Appleton-Century Crofts.

Slabakova, R. (2009). Features or parameters: Which one makes SLA easier, and more interesting to study? *Second Language Research*, 25, 313–324.

Stowe, L. A., Haverkort, M., and Zwarts, F. (2005). Rethinking the neurological basis of language. *Lingua*, 115, 997–1042

Swain, M., (1985). Communicative competence: Some roles of comprehensible input and comprehensible output in its development. In S. Gass and C. Madden (eds), *Input in Second Language Acquisition*. Rowley, MA: Newbury House Publishers, Inc.

Swain, M. (1995). Three functions of output in second language learning. In G. Cook and B. Seidlhofer (eds), *Principles and Practice in Applied Linguistics* (pp. 125–144). Oxford: Oxford University Press.

Swain, M. (1998). Focus on form through conscious reflection. In C. Doughty and J. Williams (eds), *Focus on Form in Classroom Second Language Acquisition* (pp. 64–81). New York: Cambridge University Press.

Swain, M. (2005). The output hypothesis: Theory and research. In Hinkel, E. (ed.), *Handbook of Research in Second Language Teaching and Learning* (pp. 471–483). Mahwah, NJ: Lawrence Erlbaum Associates.

Swain, M., and Lapkin, S., (1995). Problems in output and the cognitive process they generate: A step towards second language learning. *Applied Linguistics*, 16, 371–391.

Tomlin, R., and Villa, V. (2004). Attention in cognitive science and second language acquisition. *Studies in Second Language Acquisition*, 16, 183–204.

Truscott, J., and Sharwood Smith, M. (2004). Acquisition by processing: A modular perspective on language development. *Language and Cognition*, 7, 1–20.

Tsimpli, I. M, and Roussou, A. (1991). Parameter-resetting in L2? *UCL Working Papers in Linguistics* 3, 149–70

Ullman, M. (2001). The declarative/procedural model of lexicon and grammar. *Journal of Psycholinguistic Research*, 30, 37–69.

Ullman, M. (2015). The declarative/procedural model: A neurobiologically motivated theory of first and second language. In B. VanPatten and J. Williams (eds), *Theories in Second Language Acquisition* (2nd ed.; pp. 135–158). New York: Routledge.

Vainikka A., and Young-Scholten M. (1996. Gradual development of L2 phrase structure. *Second Language Research*, 12, 7–39.

Valdés, G. (2001). Heritage Language Students: Profiles and Possibilities. In J. Peyton, J. Ranard and S. McGinnis (eds), *Heritage Languages in America: Preserving a National Resource* (pp. 37–80). McHenry, IL: The Center for Applied Linguistics and Delta Systems.

Valdés, G. (2005). Bilingualism, heritage language learners, and SLA research: Opportunities lost or seized? *The Modern Language Journal*, 89, 410–426.

VanPatten, B. (1996). *Input Processing and Grammar Instruction: Theory and Research*. Norwood, NJ: Ablex.

VanPatten, B. (2003). *From Input to Output: A Teacher's Guide to Second Language Acquisition*. New York: McGraw-Hill.

VanPatten, B. (ed.) (2004). *Processing Instruction: Theory, Research, and Commentary*. Mahwah, NJ: Lawrence Erlbaum Associates.

VanPatten, B. (2010). The two faces of SLA: Mental representation and skill. *International Journal of English Language Studies*, 10, 1–18.

VanPatten, B. (2014). Creating comprehensible input and output. Fundamental Considerations in Language Learning. *The Language Education*, 24–26.

VanPatten, B. (2015). Input processing in adult SLA. In B. VanPatten and J. Williams (eds), *Theories in Second Language Acquisition* (2nd ed.; pp. 113–135). New York: Routledge.

VanPatten, B., and Benati, A. (2010). *Key Terms in Second Language Acquisition*. London: Continuum.

VanPatten, B., and Benati, A. (2015). *Key Terms in Second Language Acquisition* (2nd ed.). London: Bloomsbury.

VanPatten, B., and Rothman, J. (2013). Against rules. In A. Benati, C. Laval and M. Arche (eds), *The Grammar Dimension in Instructed Second Language*

Learning: Advances in Instructed Second Language Acquisition Research
(pp. 15–35). Bloomsbury Academic, London.

VanPatten, B., and Williams, J. (eds), (2015). *Theories in Second Language Acquisition* (2nd ed.). New York: Routledge.

VanPatten, B., Williams, J., Rott, S., and Overstreet, M. (eds), (2004). *Form–Meaning Connections in Second Language Acquisition*. Mahwah, NJ: Lawrence Erlbaum Associates.

Vetter, E. (2012). Multilingualism pedagogy: building bridges between languages. In J. Hüttner, B. Schiftner, B. Mehlmauer, and S. Reichl (eds), *Theory and Practice in EFL Teacher Education: Bridging the Gap* (pp. 228–246). Bristol: Multilingual Matters.

Vygotsky, L. S. (1978). *Mind in Society: The Development of Higher Psychological Processes*. Cambridge, MA: Harvard University Press.

Wei, L. (2000). *The Bilingual Reader*. London: Routledge.

Weinreich, U. (1953). *Languages in Contact: Findings and Problems*. New York: Linguistic Circle of New York.

White, L. (1985). The pro-drop parameter in adult second language acquisition. *Language Learning*, 35, 47–62.

White, L. (1989). *Universal Grammar and Second Language Acquisition*. Amsterdam: John Benjamins Publishing.

White, L. (1996). Universal grammar and second language acquisition: Current trends and new directions. In W. Ritchie and T. Bhatia (eds), *Handbook of Language Acquisition* (pp. 85–120). New York: Academic Press.

White, L. (2003). *Second Language Acquisition and Universal Grammar*. Cambridge: Cambridge University Press.

White, L. (2015). Linguistic theory, universal grammar, and second language acquisition. In B. VanPatten and J. Williams (eds), *Theories in Second Language Acquisition* (2nd ed.; pp. 34–53). New York: Routledge.

White, L., and Genesee, F. (1996). How native is near-native? The issue of ultimate attainment in adult second language acquisition. *Second Language Research*, 12, 233–365.

Widdowson, H. G. (1983). *Learning Purpose and Language Use*. Oxford: Oxford University Press.

Williams, J. (2005). *Teaching Writing in Second and Foreign Language Classrooms*. NJ: McGraw-Hill.

Wong, W. (2005). *Input Enhancement: From Theory and Research to the Classroom*. New York: McGraw-Hill.

Yule, G. and Tarone, E. (1997). Investigating communication strategies in L2 reference: Pros and cons. In G. Kasper and E. Kellerman (eds), *Communication Strategies: Psycholinguistic and Sociolinguistic Perspectives* (pp. 17–30). New York: Longman.

Zobl, H. (1981). Markedness and the projection problem. *Language Learning*, 33, 293–313.

Index